# THE REVOLUTION IN PHILOSOPHY

# THE REVOLUTION
# IN PHILOSOPHY

BY

A. J. AYER

W. C. KNEALE · G. A. PAUL

D. F. PEARS · P. F. STRAWSON

G. J. WARNOCK · R. A. WOLLHEIM

WITH AN INTRODUCTION

BY

GILBERT RYLE

LONDON

MACMILLAN & CO LTD

NEW YORK · ST MARTIN'S PRESS

1957

MACMILLAN AND COMPANY LIMITED
*London Bombay Calcutta Madras Melbourne*

THE MACMILLAN COMPANY OF CANADA LIMITED
*Toronto*

ST MARTIN'S PRESS INC
*New York*

PRINTED IN GREAT BRITAIN

# CONTENTS

# INTRODUCTION

THE wise rambler occasionally, though not incessantly, looks back over his shoulder in order to link up the place he has got to with the country through which he has recently passed. It is equally wise for thinkers occasionally, though not incessantly, to try to fix in retrospect the courses that they have followed and the positions from which they have moved.

A good view of our own proximate origins we cannot get. History begins only when memory's dust has settled. Yesterday's ways of thinking and living are too continuous with the ways in which we think and live today for us to see them clearly. None the less, attempts to trace our proximate origins, though premature as history, are valuable in three ways. Like memoirs, they supply the future historian with those considered and marshalled reminiscences which he will need. Like sketch-maps, they improve their authors' own senses of direction. Like reports of Royal Commissions, they help the student to understand the contemporary scene — partly by disabusing him of fashionable misconceptions of what is going on.

In introducing this series of lectures, I have three main things to do. First I shall sketch the shape of the social and cultural stage on which have been performed the philosophical scenes that the seven lecturers describe. Then I shall suggest the plot, or some strands of the plot that runs through these scenes. Finally, I shall mention a few other philosophical events which, though deliberately passed over in this series of lectures, still need to be remembered by anyone who wants his survey to be inclusive.

1. Between the time when Bradley was an undergraduate and the time when I was an undergraduate the population of intellectuals, and particularly of academic intellectuals in the British Isles had changed from being a predominantly clerical to an almost entirely lay population. In Bradley's youth most Fellows of colleges were in orders, and a big proportion of the undergraduates came from, and were destined to go to, the vicarage or the manse. The burning theoretical issues were between theologians and theologians, or else between theologians and anti-theologians. Beneath and behind even the more purely philosophical divisions of opinion there commonly lay the division between faith and doubt. By the 1920's all of this had gone. Almost all university teachers were laymen ; almost all undergraduates came from lay homes and looked forward to secular careers. A philosophy tutor had for his daily companions researchers in the natural and the applied sciences, in mathematics, in ancient and modern history, in economics and law, in ancient, modern, and oriental languages and literature. He might not have among his colleagues one theologian. The fires of philosophical theology and anti-theology were already burning low by the last decade or two

2

of the nineteenth century; by the time that I first attended philosophical discussions, in the middle 1920's, they were out. In their stead there had sprung up many other intellectual interests. Lecture halls, laboratories, and common-rooms were occupied by theoretical discussions of new kinds. The theoretical imbroglios that stimulate philosophy came out of the work not of Renan, Newman, or Colenso, but of such people as Cantor, Clark Maxwell, Mendel, Karl Marx, Frazer, and Freud.

There was another thing at work during this period which powerfully affected both the topics dealt with by philosophers and the manners in which they dealt with them. Philosophy developed into a separate academic subject, partly detached from classical scholarship, from theology, from economics, and last of all from psychology. The teachers of philosophy of an university came to constitute a faculty, and they organized their own discussion-groups. From 1876 there existed the quarterly journal *Mind*, and not very much later there was formed The Aristotelian Society, at the meetings of which were read and discussed papers that were subsequently printed in the Society's annual proceedings. Where Mill, Huxley, and Leslie Stephen had published their philosophical articles in the ordinary Reviews, Bradley, Moore, and Russell published theirs in the philosophers' professional organ or in the Proceedings of the philosophers' metropolitan forum. This new professional practice of submitting problems and arguments to the expert criticism of fellow craftsmen led to a growing concern with questions of philosophical technique and a

3

growing passion for ratiocinative rigour. Eloquence will not silence rival experts and edification is not palatable to colleagues. Nor is the span of an article or a discussion-paper broad enough to admit of a crusade against, or a crusade on behalf of, any massive 'Ism'. Philosophers had now to be philosophers' philosophers; and in their colloquia there was as little room for party politics as there is in courts of law. From both these causes transcendental dictions were becoming unidiomatic at the same time as the technicalities of logical theory and scientific method were stiffening the working parlance of philosophers. This laicizing of our culture and this professionalizing of philosophy together explain much of the change in style and direction of philosophy in (roughly) the post-Victorian English-speaking world. Bradley straddled the period of transition.

2 (a) Consequently the moment could not be long delayed when philosophers would challenge one another, and be challenged by their new academic colleagues, especially the natural scientists, to state unequivocally what sort of an enquiry philosophy was and what were the canons of its special methods, if it possessed any such methods. Already surrendering its historic linkage with 'mental science' or psychology, and no longer remembering its former claim to be the science of things transcendental, philosophy looked like losing its credentials as a science of anything at all. This challenge was made all the more serious by the rapid advance of studies in the logic of mathematics, the logic of probable and statistical reasoning, the logic of induction and the

4

methodology of the social sciences. The era which produced Boole, de Morgan, Mill, Jevons, Frege, Venn, Bradley, Peirce, Russell, and Whitehead had been equipping itself with criteria of cogency which philosophical thinking would find it hard to satisfy. Sterile of demonstrable theorems, sterile of experimentally testable hypotheses, philosophy was to face the charge of being sterile.

It is, therefore, no freak of history that the example and the reputation of Moore's analytic method of philosophizing proved so influential; since here was a philosopher practising a specific method of investigation, with obviously high standards of strictness. It is no freak of history that the iconoclasm of the Vienna Circle shook the equanimity of philosophers, since though they were already half alive to the truth, they were not alive to all the implications of the truth, that as their procedures were not scientific procedures, so their answers to their questions and even their questions were not scientific.

It is, again, no freak of history that Wittgenstein, in his *Tractatus*, was concerned, perhaps above all else, to show how the propositions of Formal Logic and, derivatively, those of philosophy are condemned to be uninformative about the world and yet able, in some important way, to be clarificatory of those propositions that are informative about the world, reporting no matters of fact yet correcting our mishandlings of reported matters of fact. For Formal Logic, no less than philosophy, failed to satisfy the newly formulated requirements of either a deductive or an inductive science. It is, lastly, through no perversity that the two last lectures of this present series are enquiries into the nature of philosophical enquiry; since just this seemingly domestic issue has for some thirty years inevitably been a preoccupation of English-speaking philosophers.

(*b*) The life-span of Bradley coincided almost exactly with that of Frege, namely from the middle 1840's to the middle 1920's. Had they anything else in common? First, both were in revolt against 'psychologism', in revolt, that is, against one dominant element in the teachings of John Stuart Mill. Mill, transmitting the legacy of Hume, had tended to treat problems of logic and epistemology as problems to be solved by associationist psychology. Frege and Bradley in different ways and with different emphases distinguished sharply between psychology on the one side and philosophy and logic on the other; between the ideas, impressions, and feelings that were the subject matter of psychology and whatever it was that formed the subject matters of philosophy and logic.

Next, both detected the same philosophical superstition behind the associationist account of thoughts, namely the assumption that any thought (or judgement or proposition) is a concatenation of separately existing and separately inspectable pieces. The traditional analysis of a judgement into detachable terms, occasionally and temporarily harnessed together by a supervenient copula, was the mould of which Mill's chemistry of idea-compounds was only a new-fangled filling. Against this false psychology and against the underlying assumption that terms are prior to propositions, both Frege and Bradley maintained that a thought or judgement is a functional unity, possessing, of course, distinguishable features but not composed out of detachable pieces. The copula is not a coupling-chain. The verb in a statement needs its nouns and adjectives no more than they need it.

Next, both recognized that judgements or propositions are not all of the one hallowed subject-predicate pattern and that arguments are not all of the syllogistic pattern. The verb 'is' of *Socrates is a man* is not privileged above all other verbs. Logic has to study manifold differences of logical form, not to iron out these differences.

Next, both saw that it is not extrinsic but intrinsic to a thought to be true or false, or to have 'objective reference'. When I judge, I judge that something is the case. If it is not the case, then I have misjudged; and the allegation that I have misjudged implies that something else is the case. In saying what we think, we do not just signal what is going on in our heads; we describe, or else we misdescribe reality. The associationist psychology had seemed to reduce a piece of thinking to the occurring of an introspectible idea or gaggle of ideas, leaving no place for the mission or occupation of these ideas. Describing thinking without mentioning what makes it successful or else unsuccessful thinking, is like describing the batsman's movements without mentioning the bowling.

Finally, in the hands of both Frege and Bradley the notion of Meaning became, what it has remained ever since, an indispensable, if refractory, instrument of philosophical discourse. Logicians and philosophers no more examine the private and momentary images and impressions that are the material of psychology, than they examine the English or Russian phrases or sentences that are the material of philology. In investigating the structure of thoughts they are investigating what these ideas and these dictions *mean*. The distinction between the vehicle and what it conveys is what distinguishes factual enquiries, like psychology and philology, from conceptual enquiries, like logic and philosophy. It is because our dictions have sense or, as Bradley less naturally says, because our images have meanings, that what we think is capable of being true or false of reality and capable of implying and being incompatible with other judgements about reality.

The story of twentieth-century philosophy is very largely the story of this notion of sense or meaning. Meanings (to use a trouble-making plural noun) are what Moore's analyses have been analyses of; meanings are what Russell's logical atoms were atoms of; meanings, in one sense but not in another, were what Russell's 'incomplete symbols' were bereft of; meanings are what logical considerations prohibit to the antinomy-generating forms of words on which Frege and Russell had tried to found arithmetic; meanings are what the members of the Vienna Circle proffered a general litmus-paper for; meanings are what the *Tractatus*, with certain qualifications, denies to the would-be propositions both of Formal Logic and of philosophy; and yet meanings are just what, in different ways, philosophy and logic are *ex officio* about.

3. A comprehensive survey of twentieth-century

philosophy in the English-speaking world certainly have to take account of some influences which could not be dealt with in this series of lectures. First, the pragmatism of James was one minor source of the Principle of Verifiability. More important was his influence upon psychology. He, with Galton, in the English-speaking world, transplanted psychology from the study to the laboratory and thus, un-intentionally, forced philosophers and psychologists to cease thinking of 'mental science' as a label covering both of their subjects. But I suspect that James' biggest influence will turn out to be this. He restored to philosophy, what had been missing since Hume, that sense of the ridiculous which saves one from taking seriously everything that is said solemnly. James brought back the pinch of salt.

Next, Brentano's pupil, Meinong, also in mutiny against Mill, developed an ultra Platonic theory of Meanings which, by its very thoroughness, jerked Russell and others out of a seductive blind alley.

Next, some of the technical or semi-technical ideas on which the new Formal Logic was based were taken over by philosophers for the solution of their own problems. One conspicuous instance of this tendency is the way in which the notion of *relation* was seized upon. This notion achieved logical respectability with de Morgan; and relational inferences were codified in Russell's *Principles of Mathematics* (1903). The potentialities of the *xRy* propositional pattern, as against those of the overworked *s-p* pattern, were soon highly esteemed by philosophers, who hoped by means of it to bring to order all sorts of recalcitrances in the notions of knowing, believing, perceiving, remembering, imagining, wanting, meaning, and many others. A lot of these hopes were disappointed. The new groove was not much more efficacious than the old. But from the exercise of leaving the old and trying out the new groove much was learned.

A second instance came from the calculus of propositions. The codification of the conjunctions *and*, *or*, and *if*, together with *not*, brought under control a variety of kinds of compound or 'molecular' propositions. This encouraged Russell (intermittently), Wittgenstein, and the Vienna Circle to think of the analysis of meanings less as the analysis of complex concepts into their simple component concepts, than as the analysis of compound propositions into their simple elements, the conjunctionless or 'atomic' propositions. The goal of analysis was no longer to isolate simple name-ables, but to isolate simple stateables. To explicate is not to give the final definition of a complex predicate, but to give all the truth-conditions of a complex statement. The verbal expression of even an 'atom' of meaning would always require the presence of a live verb. Sense and senselessness belong where truth and falsity belong, namely to complete sentences or statements. The meanings of subordinate parts of speech are abstracted features of what is or might be conveyed by full sentences, not pieces out of which the meanings of sentences are composed. The philosophical scent given by the logically disciplined conjunctions soon petered out, and the ultimates of Logical Atomism took sanctuary in Utopia. But the chase had blown away at least one bad dream. There must be many other tributary influences, of no less importance, that I have failed to mention.

The fact that philosophers have become more secular in their interests, more technical in their discourse, and more self-conscious about the nature of their own calling does not by itself involve that they have become better at their jobs than their predecessors had been. The sophistication of the virtuoso does not make him a master. Yet sophistication, though not sufficient, is still necessary for progress.

It has not been part of the task of these seven lecturers to describe the contemporary happenings whose origins they have tried to trace. But, in this introduction, it needs to be mentioned that there is now in progress vigorous movement in various stretches of the philosophical water. In ethics, epistemology, the philosophy of mind, the philosophy of language, philosophical jurisprudence, the philosophy of science, aesthetics, and philosophical scholarship, radical problems are being tackled in partly new ways. Whether much or little progress has been made by the philosophical thinking that has been going on since our recent sophistication began, will be for later generations to judge.

# F. H. BRADLEY

FRANCIS HERBERT BRADLEY was born in 1846 and died in 1924. In 1870 he was elected a Fellow of Merton College, Oxford, and most of his life was spent within its precincts. He was permanently a sick man, and never lectured, and never taught. He wrote four books, and many articles. The burden of his metaphysical thought is contained in *The Principles of Logic*, which appeared in 1883; *Appearance and Reality* of 1893; and *Essays on Truth and Reality* of 1914. All are written in the same highly personal, highly nervous style, full of caustic epigrams and poetic metaphors, the natural vehicle of a cruel tongue and an ardent imagination.

In the history of philosophy, Bradley is in one tradition and, more self-consciously, outside another. The tradition to which he belongs is that of Idealist philosophy, the tradition fundamentally of Hegel and of his German successors such as Lotze and Sigwart. The tradition to which he does not belong is the native English empiricist tradition, the tradition of Locke, Berkeley, Hume, and John Stuart Mill — to name its most obvious adherents. In Bradley's case it is the nonconformity that is more important than the conformity. 'As for the "Hegelian School" which exists in our reviews,' he wrote, 'I know of no one who has met with it anywhere else.' [1] But as for the school of 'Experience', as he mockingly called it, Bradley not only knew of its existence, not only disagreed with its tenets, but felt for them a combination of contempt and loathing.

Much of Bradley's philosophical thought is very abstract and very obscure, and to attempt to summarize it would be vain. In this talk I wish to discuss only two elements in it, both of which were in flagrant contradiction to accepted English ideas : that is to say, the separation of logic and philosophy from psychology, and monism, the theory that Reality is an indivisible whole. In Bradley's thought there is clearly an intimate connection between these two theses, as I shall try to show. But, for all that, they are different : for, as will emerge in later talks, subsequent philosophers have almost universally subscribed to the former thesis and all have unanimously dissented from the latter.

To understand Bradley's severance of logic or philosophy from psychology, we need to go back somewhat in time : to the late seventeenth century. For it was Locke who with his 'new way of ideas' set English philosophy on the path that it was to follow for the next two hundred years. For him philosophy, as for most philosophers, was the study of the foundations of human knowledge. Human knowledge was what was or what could be in the human mind. The contents of the human mind were exclusively discrete ideas, occurring in time, and the operations of the mind were exclusively combinations

[1] F. H. Bradley, *The Principles of Logic*, 2nd ed. (London, 1922) vol. i, p. x.

of these ideas. Accordingly, the task of philosophy was, first, to trace these ideas to their origin : and, secondly, to expound the exact nature of their combinations. Generally, ideas seem to have been equated with mental images ; but, in any case, what was indubitable was that philosophy studied actual mental phenomena, psychical facts, something that occurred like a sensation or emotion.

All this Bradley rejected. 'In England', he wrote, 'we have lived too long in the psychological attitude.'[1] What he intended by this may be brought out by considering the simple case of someone thinking about a horse. To the empiricist philosopher, this is roughly equivalent to his entertaining in his mind an image of a horse. But to Bradley such a view misses the real point. For even if it is true that whenever we, say, think about a horse, we do have a mental image of a horse, thinking cannot be just having that image. It is, rather, using that image to refer to other objects. Any mental image we may describe. In doing so, we describe what it is. But apart from this, there is also what it means : and what it means is always something other than what it is. Accordingly, if philosophy is interested in discussing images from the point of view of what they mean, this is in no way achieved by an investigation of what they are. And what is true of images is true of all other mental occurrences. Put generally, the idea that psychology studies is not the same as the idea that philosophy or logic studies. Hence the two subjects are quite different.

[1] F. H. Bradley, *The Principles of Logic*, 2nd ed. (London, 1922) vol. i, p. 2.

The severance of philosophy and logic from psychology is, as I have already said, common to Bradley and nearly all his successors however many differences may keep them apart. The consequences of it are manifold. It involves a new conception of the traditional Laws of Thought. It leads to the adoption of a new starting-point in philosophy : the judgement or proposition, instead of the idea or the concept. It sharpens an interest in necessary truths.

But here I want to stress only two aspects of it, both of which are important for Bradley's monism. For in contrast to the psychologist's idea, which is a particular, specific, psychic fact, the idea that the philosopher should study is necessarily general : for an idea regarded as possessing a meaning is a sign of some species, kind, or class. And again, whereas the idea as studied by the psychologist is something natural, belonging to the natural history of the mind, the idea as studied by the philosopher is an artifact ; the result of something that we do to, some process to which we submit the ordinary existent empirical phenomena of the mind.

Now it is the universality and the factitiousness of ideas that intensify for Bradley the problem to which Monism is, on several counts, considered the only satisfactory answer : the relation of Thought to Reality.

For the empiricists there had, by and large, been no such general problem. Admittedly there were for them certain kinds of occasion on which the relation was not clear : when, say, we attribute powers or causal properties to objects, though we can never observe such forces ; or when we talk about all objects of a certain kind, whereas our experience can never be so general. But there was one sort of occasion on which the relation was quite clear : when, so to say, the two are face to face, when, confronted by a particular isolated event or fact, we describe it. And this being so, there was hope for the other occasions. For might it not be possible in some way, with sufficient ingenuity, to reduce what we do on these other occasions to what we do on the occasion when all is transparent ?

And yet just where there were said to be no difficulties, Bradley saw them. He said that we can never talk about isolated events. And, worse still, he said that there were no such things.

Let us take the sort of case where it seems most plausible to say that we are talking about isolated events. Let us imagine that I am standing in a field and I see a brown bird and I say 'The bird is brown'. Here, surely, I am describing some particular, isolated fact, and describing it truly. But, for Bradley, this is not so clear. For there are many birds and many of them are not brown : some are yellow, some black, some white, some strange exotic colours — and my judgement seems to range over all of them, and to most of them be false. For it to be particular and true, I must pin it down to the actual bird now flying overhead.

Can I ever do this ? Now, one way in which we might think we could secure this coveted uniqueness is to insert into our judgement more and more descriptions of the bird in question. But though Bradley admits that these would be steps in the right direction, they can never bring us to our destination.

For whatever descriptions we insert, there is always the chance that there is some other bird that they also fit : and so this one here and now, is not singled out. The generality of language is our undoing.

But, then, we might ask, why not do what I have just done : that is, use words such as 'this' and 'here' and 'now' to pin our judgement on to the particular object before us. But, according to Bradley, if we try to do this we fare no better. We abandon one type of generality, that of description, only to accept one that is more embracing, that of demonstratives. For it is clear that everything, at one time, from one position, is correctly called 'here' and 'now'. If we try to specify the time and the position from which we are actually speaking, we are back in the world of descriptions.

The moral that Bradley draws from this is that our only way of securing uniqueness is to specify the relations of our object with all other objects in the world, past, present, and future, actual and imagined : and to do this is, of course, to introduce the whole of Reality.

The assumptions that lie behind this argument are interesting because they are shared by many of Bradley's successors. They amount in effect to a view of the working of language. According to it sentences fasten on to the world, refer to the world, solely in virtue of the meaning that they in themselves possess ; if, that is, they do so at all. Such a view is, I suggest, peculiarly a logician's view, because it treats all sentences as being on a level with the examples that appear in text-books of logic. Let me explain. We read, for instance, on page 80 of Quine's *Methods of Logic* the sentence, 'Some of the witnesses are employees'. And this might, this could tantalize us. We might ask, 'But in what case?' 'Employees of whom?' 'What was the charge?' And not getting an answer, we might say, 'I don't see what this sentence refers to. It's hopelessly vague.'

But, of course, this would be absurd, because the sentence is not being used to refer to any particular occasion at all. If it were so used, then the object of its reference would be secured for it not solely by its meaning but also by the speaker's intention. And the speaker in deciding whether a particular expression was or was not adequate to convey his intentions, would take into account the listener's expectations. What is characteristic of Bradley's view is that it ignores the whole context in which words are used. It treats them not as arrows that we, the marksmen, aim at targets: but as missiles that take themselves there, or fall wide of the mark.

But this argument about 'designation' or 'uniqueness' is by no means the full burden of Bradley's criticism of the particular judgement; or even its most impressive part. He goes on to argue that even if we could secure uniqueness for our judgement, if we could pin it down to the particular fact, it would do violence to the fact. For the judgement cuts up the fact, it dissects it. It severs, say, the brownness of the bird from the bird itself: but as in Reality they are together, the judgement is thereby unfaithful to Reality. 'It is a very common and most ruinous superstition to suppose that analysis is no alteration.' [1]

[1] F. H. Bradley, *The Principles of Logic*, 2nd ed. (London, 1922) vol. i, p. 95.

To establish this point, Bradley bids us consider the one-ness of what we experience in the immediacy of feeling. There is diversity there, but not division. The divisions come only when we begin to reflect, to apply concepts and words to experience; and concepts and words are artificial implements; for, as we have seen, it is we who make ideas in the philosopher's sense out of ideas in the psychological sense.

And once we have in this way carved up the experience of the moment, severed the qualities and relations from the subject, the brownness of the bird from the bird itself, nothing we do, Bradley argues, can ever put it together again. Experience now lies in a multitude of small, different pieces, and when we try, for instance, to say, 'The bird is brown', we utter a falsehood: because in thought we have already separated, severed the bird from its brownness. By now, one *just is not* the other.

Bradley was surely right in emphasizing, as opposed to the empiricists, the artificial character of language, the way it acts as a grid that we place over Reality. For they in their *naïveté* had believed that once we analyse our ideas into their constituent elements, the simple ideas into which the others can be resolved correspond directly to the simple elements of which the world is composed. But in emphasizing the grid-like character of language, Bradley suggests too crude a picture of the grid. He argues as though its meshes were all of the same kind, and hence that all the pieces are of the same shape, and so can only lie side by side, disconnected. It is as if in making a jigsaw puzzle, we made all the pieces, say, perfect squares. And then the question would legitimately arise, How can they ever interlock?

But Bradley can scarcely be blamed for treating the judgement or proposition as a mere bag of homogeneous terms. This view had been universal amongst philosophers, at least since the seventeenth century, and Bradley at least had the insight to see the intolerable difficulties to which it gave rise. These can be removed only by a subtler analysis of the function of the sentence or statement in binding terms together into a whole. Such an analysis we now possess in the form of the propositional function, and for this we are indebted to the insight of later logicians.

It is clear that Bradley's attack on the particular judgement goes beyond its objective. For in criticizing the way we try to distinguish between the related elements within the experience of the moment, Bradley is in effect impugning all attempts to divide up Reality. For do we not ordinarily think that every event is related to every other event : at least in the all but trivial way of being spatially or temporally related? If so, then by what *right* do we regard any event in isolation from any other? If Bradley is correct in saying that we ought not to split up the moment internally, the brownness of the bird from the bird, the bird from the tree, then equally we ought not to split up any moment from what happens anywhere else at that moment, or anywhere at any other moment. To consider anything, we must consider everything.

There are other arguments that Bradley uses to show the error that infects any attempt to take in isolation what common sense regards as 'isolated facts' : say, the bird on the tree in Hampshire, and the death of a Roman gladiator. Some of these arguments are obscure ; and others — such as that which invokes the fact that everything is causally connected with everything else — seem more consonant with his opponents' outlook than with his own. But for the most part, they relate to the incompatibility of Thought and Reality, which, in turn, arises from the way in which Thought makes divisions where none exist in Reality.

To recapitulate Bradley's arguments about the particular judgement, we may observe that at times he seems to be saying that, owing to the universality of language, the particular judgement is a destination at which we can never arrive, and at other times that it is no real destination, but a mirage for which the artificality of language is responsible. It is, of course, this second line of criticism that is more fundamental, obliterating as it does the ideal to which so much of our thought and science and literature is directed : the transfixing of the isolated fact, like a butterfly, on the pin of language.

What does Bradley offer us in its place ? The reconstruction of thought that according to him is necessary, if we are to slough the errors of our ordinary ways of thinking, takes place in two stages. The first stage demands that we must cease thinking of the world as consisting entirely of objects that possess certain properties, that stand in certain relations to other objects, but that could possess other properties, could be differently related to other objects, and yet be the same ; we must not think, for instance, that the bird before us, brown, sitting on the bough,

21

could be black and flying across the sky, and yet be the same bird.

In logic this view is known as the theory of 'internal relations'. All the relations in which an object stands are rooted in its nature as firmly as triangularity is rooted in the nature of the triangle. And Bradley held this to be no more than a rigorous formulation of the truism that relations make a difference to the things they relate. If my chair is to the north of my desk, this may be an unimportant fact about it : but still it makes a difference to it, my chair would not be just the same if it were to the east of my desk. And to this the reply can be made, Yes, of course, being to the north of my desk makes a difference to my chair : but only this difference — that it makes it to the north of my desk and not elsewhere. It doesn't affect its *other* properties, its essential properties. But to this sort of objection, which was later to be urged against his theory, Bradley was always alive ; and forearmed against it. It was fallacious, according to him to argue that such a relation as 'being to the north of my desk' makes a difference to my chair only in that it makes a difference to its spatial properties, but that it makes no difference to its other properties ; for, he argued, just this way of looking at objects is already vicious. For, in Bradley's view, we ought not to ask whether any relation makes a difference to an object regarded as having these properties, or those properties, seen as a kind of thing or 'character', but we ought to ask about it not in this abstract fashion but as a particular existing thing. And if we are to do justice to his view and to see where it goes wrong, we need,

I suggest, a more penetrating analysis of the way we refer to objects than any that Bradley's critics have produced. We need to show how we refer to objects sometimes by describing such characteristics as they possess, but sometimes, it seems, by names or demonstratives aimed at their very heart. We refer to a desk as '*this* desk'. Though the expression does not mean all the properties that this desk possesses, by our expression we *mean a* desk which does in fact possess them all.

But, of course, a point of view that sees all relations as internal cannot be the final resting-point for Bradley: for it still preserves the notion of terms and relations, though the terms are now inseparable, and the relations are internal. Bradley offers a higher reconstruction yet, in which all the wounds inflicted by thought on reality heal over. Subjects and their properties, terms and their relations, and even in some mysterious fashion, thought and reality coalesce: the old immediacy of feeling is restored, though on a higher level. This obscure condition, known to Bradley as the Absolute, is clearly the death of thought, though also, he assures us, its consummation: and so it is not surprising that it cannot be precisely or even comprehensibly described in thought as we know it.

In our effort to understand these two stages of reconditioned thought, we may find analogy helpful: in each case, analogy drawn from the sphere of art. The view of the world as a necessary system may be compared to one ideal of the aesthetic critic, as Bradley himself suggests. For in looking at a work of art, particularly a work of visual art, we are often so susceptible to the importance of unity, that we choose to see the parts as gaining their significance from the way they minister to it. It is possible, of course, for part of a canvas to be mutilated and the rest remain intact, but what remains we see as altered. Or again in looking at a picture, we may concentrate on a hand or a fold of the drapery, but as long as we know that this is only a detail, we see it as different from what it would be if we took it for the whole.

The analogy for the final stage of Bradley's thought is to be found, if it can be found at all, perhaps in the vision of the artist himself. Sometimes we find in the work of the greatest artists ordered systems such as I have just described, which yet seem to suggest that they have for their inspiration some experience in which there was diversity but no separateness, immediacy and yet high intelligence. And to those rare and strange moments we encounter sometimes in their letters or autobiographical notes testimony necessarily as obscure as it is precious.

So Rilke, for example :

He recalled the time in that other southern garden (Capri), when a bird-call in the open and in his inner consciousness were one, when it did not, as it were, break on the barrier of his body, but gathered both together into an undivided space, in which there was only one region of the purest, deepest consciousness, mysteriously protected. On that occasion he had closed his eyes, so that he might not be confused by the contour of the body in such a generously granted experience, and infinity passed into him from all sides in so familiar a manner that he could believe he felt within him the gentle presence of the stars which had now appeared.[1]

But to end on this note would be misleading, for it would give us a picture of Bradley as a philosopher who turned his back on the world as *we* know it, who advised men to drop their ordinary ways of thought and follow his. And he was nothing of the sort. It is true that he set out to subject those very general beliefs and opinions about the character of the world which secure widespread acceptance and the philosophy that is thought to embody them if in a more systematic form, to a test that he said no reasonable man could deny; and that these beliefs failed to pass this test, and that Bradley concluded from this that ultimate truth lay elsewhere.

But at no moment did Bradley reject these beliefs. He admitted that in their way they were perfectly adequate. Only they answered to different and lower needs. Ultimately Bradley believed that there was no conflict between Science and Metaphysics, just as some theologians of the period had satisfied themselves that there was no conflict between Science and Religion. To many at the time the gaining of such an assurance must have seemed an overwhelming triumph. Within a few years it was to be counted a Pyrrhic victory. By placing Metaphysics beyond the bounds of criticism Bradley placed it beyond the pale of belief.

[1] Rainer Maria Rilke, *Selected Works* : vol. i, *Prose*, trans. by G. Craig Houston (Hogarth Press, 1954), p. 36.

# GOTTLOB FREGE
## AND MATHEMATICAL LOGIC

GOTTLOB FREGE was born in 1848, lived a
quiet life as a teacher of mathematics in the
University of Jena, and died in 1925. At the
time of his death I was an undergraduate, already
interested in logic, and I think that I should have
taken notice if there had been any speeches made or
articles published that year in his honour. But I
can recollect nothing of the kind; and I believe that
at that time few philosophers had any inkling of the
fact that as far back as 1879, in a pamphlet called
*Begriffsschrift* (that is, Ideography or Concept-script),
Frege had produced the first complete system of
formal logic. This is not to say that his ideas had
been entirely neglected in his lifetime. On the
contrary, they had won great triumphs among
mathematicians and philosophers through *Principia
Mathematica*, the famous work of Whitehead and
Russell, which appeared first in 1910 and reached
a second edition in the year of Frege's death. But
Frege's own works were not read. On all suitable
occasions Russell made generous acknowledgement
of Frege's priority in the attempt to reduce arithmetic to logic; but there was a widespread impression that it was not worth while to read Frege's
own writings, and so the greatness of his achieve-

ment was not realized in his lifetime. How this came about we shall see presently. Let us try first to get clear what he had in mind and what he did towards carrying out his project.

Perhaps it will be best to begin by reminding ourselves of some of the perplexities we felt when we learnt algebra at school. You may remember being puzzled about minus numbers. Perhaps you said to the mathematics master, 'How can $-2$ be a number?' and he tried to set your mind at rest by telling you that talk of minus two was something like the recording of a debt. Or perhaps you were worried about $\sqrt{2}$, and wondered how that could possibly be a number, if, as the master said, it could never be written down in the form of a completed decimal. Or you may have gone farther and racked your brains over $\sqrt{-1}$. If you asked any such questions, you were in good company. For during the nineteenth century some of the greatest mathematicians spent a lot of time and energy in trying to find the answers to these puzzles.

In the rapid development of mathematics during the seventeenth and eighteenth centuries mathematicians had been led to make successive extensions of the number concept without any clear idea of what they were doing. At the beginning they had the notion of a natural number, that is, the sort of number you are interested in when you ask about the number of people in a family. Then they were led on to talk of negative, or minus, numbers; then after that, or about the same time, to fractions; next to irrational numbers, that is numbers like $\sqrt{2}$ which are not expressible as ratios of whole numbers;

and finally to imaginary numbers such as $\sqrt{-2}$. The names 'natural', 'integer', 'rational', and 'real' were introduced, of course, for the purpose of contrast with 'minus', 'fractional', 'irrational', and 'imaginary'. No one, for example, would wish to use the word 'real' as a name for a type of numbers until it had already become customary to speak of some other numbers as imaginary. But the scheme of classification that these names suggest is very curious. It seems as though the application of the word 'number' had been extended to wider and wider groups of objects, much as citizenship was extended in the Roman empire to wider and wider circles of humanity until in the end every free subject of the empire could claim the title. And yet this can scarcely be a good analogy. For the various recipients of Roman citizenship were all men before they became citizens, and when they became citizens they could do henceforth whatever the older citizens did. But the objects which mathematicians now dignify with the name of number are so various that it is difficult to find anything they have in common. And they certainly cannot all do the same jobs. If someone asks how many children you have, an answer such as ' $-2$ ' or ' $2/3$ ' is not merely false but senseless.

For a proper understanding of the situation we should change our analogy and think of the structure of mathematics as something like that of a mediaeval frame house in which each storey projects beyond the one below. On the ground floor we have the theory of the natural numbers. Above that, on the first floor, there is the theory of signed integers, part of which, namely the theory of positive integers, is directly above the ground floor, while the rest, the theory of negative integers, hangs in the air outside the base. Then, on the second floor, we have the theory of rational numbers, with part hanging still further out, and so on, until at the top we have the theory of complex numbers, that is, numbers of the form $x+yi$, where $i$ is $\sqrt{-1}$. The point of this analogy is that at each stage in the development of mathematics where there is said to be an extension of the number concept we have, in fact, a theory about objects of a completely new kind (on the first floor, for example, a theory of differences, on the second floor a theory of ratios, and so on), but for all that the theories hold together in an important way. Although the objects considered at the different levels are utterly different in kind, there are certain very general laws, originally formulated with reference to natural numbers, which can be re-interpreted so that they apply also to the objects of each of the successive levels. I mean the fundamental principles of algebra such as $x+y=y+x$ and $x(y+z) = xy+xz$. Furthermore, among the objects at each level there is a subset whose theory is isomorphic with the theory of the objects at the next lower level, that is to say, so exactly similar in logical pattern that for any true proposition in the one there is a single corresponding true proposition in the other. And it is only because these successive stages in the elaboration of mathematics are related in the way I have just explained, that they are all said to be concerned with numbers.

By the end of the seventies of last century all this

had been made fairly clear through the work of a number of thinkers from Gauss to Dedekind. And more than that: it had been shown that with suitable interpretations for the signs of addition and multiplication, any number of a higher level could be defined as a certain ordered set of numbers of the next lower level. Thus the theory of complex numbers had been presented by Hamilton as a theory of ordered pairs of real numbers; and a real number had been defined by Cantor as an infinite sequence of rational numbers which would ordinarily be called successive approximations to its true value; and it was not difficult to complete the process of explanation downwards through rational numbers and signed integers to the natural numbers, 1, 2, 3, etc., about which we learnt first in the infant school. This whole work of clarification was sometimes called the arithmetization of analysis. That phrase does not mean, however, that mathematical analysis, which deals with the notion of continuity, was shown to be nothing but arithmetic (for that would be absurd), but rather that it could be expounded as a theory in which no objects need be assumed except natural numbers, sets of natural numbers, sets of sets of natural numbers, and so on.

Now Frege was not satisfied with a philosophical account of mathematics that stopped there, because he wanted an explanation of the status of natural numbers. It seemed to him a scandal that no one in his day could give a sensible answer to the question, 'What is the number two?' Some said that natural numbers were mental constructs, meaning by this, apparently, that they had the same status as dreams and hallucinations. Others, again, talked as though there were no difference between numbers and the numerals by which they were represented in speech or writing. But to him it seemed clear that arithmetic was neither a branch of psychology nor a department of philology. It could, indeed, he thought, be reduced to another science, but only to logic, the bedrock of the whole edifice of mathematics.

You may perhaps be surprised that he wanted to identify arithmetic with logic; and in order to remove any possibility of misconception I must say something here about his notion of logic. He did not think of it as a study of the processes of human reasoning. On the contrary, he insisted always on the need for a sharp distinction between logic and psychology, and condemned the logic teaching of his day as *psychologisch verseucht*, that is, infected with psychology, or perhaps even more strongly, rotten with psychology. If he had lived to hear modern philosophical patter about the logic of moral language, the logic of colour words, the logic of 'God' ('God' in inverted commas, of course), I am sure that he would have been equally dissatisfied and that he would have said the science was now *philologisch verseucht*. When he wrote of logic, he meant formal logic, and he thought of this as the most general of sciences. In one place he said that it was the science of the laws of the laws of nature, and by this I think he meant that it was the science of the patterns of all thinkable states of affairs. Two hundred years earlier Leibniz had written of a *doctrina formarum*, or theory of patterns, which was to be the supreme science and to include, not only the formal logic of

the schools, but also the *ars combinatoria* that had
fascinated him while he was still in his teens. Frege
knew something of this, and he said explicitly that
his first work, the *Begriffsschrift*, was an attempt to
carry out part of Leibniz's programme.

Unfortunately, this little book has never been reprinted, so far as I know, and it is very scarce; but
some extracts from it are available in a useful volume
of *Translations from the Philosophical Writings of Gottlob
Frege*, edited by Geach and Black in 1952. The title
means literally Concept-script, and the first of the
three parts of the book is devoted to the explanation
of a new symbolism for use in studies that require
precise formulation of theses and strict derivation
from axioms. If we want to show that arithmetic is
an extension of logic, we must derive propositions
that are undoubtedly arithmetical from a base that
it is undoubtedly logical, and must do so, moreover,
without smuggling-in by the way anything taken
from experience. For this purpose, he says, we need
a symbolism that will help us to concentrate attention on what is essential for deduction, namely, the
conceptual content and its structure, as distinct from
rhetorical suggestions of all sorts. His system is
related to ordinary language, he tells us, in somewhat the same way as the microscope is related to
the eye; and it should be of service to philosophers,
because one of the tasks of philosophy is to break the
dominion of the word over human minds. Unfortunately, I cannot give you specimens of the
symbolism, because it involves arrangements of lines
in two dimensions. For the same reason it is difficult
to print, and it has been superseded in modern text-

books of logic by the notation of Peano and Russell. But I must try to explain the plan of the script.

What Frege offers is not what Leibniz called a *characteristica universalis*, that is to say, a whole new language which is supposed to help scientific thought by exhibiting the articulation of all complex ideas, but simply a version of the essential framework which must be included in our language, whatever we propose to talk about. For this purpose he uses only four basic devices. First, he has two signs which correspond more or less closely to the English words 'not' and 'if'. Next, there is a convention, taken from mathematics, whereby letters may be used to mark gaps, as for example in the formula '$x$ loves $y$', which is said to express a propositional function. When the gaps in such a formula are filled in the appropriate way, that is, by names or descriptions of individuals, the result is an expression for a proposition. And finally, he has a sign with the sense of the English word 'all', but introduced in such a way that it can be connected by a corresponding letter with any of the gaps I have just mentioned. With this rather meagre apparatus he is able to exhibit not only all the possible forms of propositions that were considered by his predecessors from Aristotle to Boole and Schröder, but also a host of others for which there was no place in the older logic, as for example the form of multiply general propositions like 'Everybody loves somebody'. It is his notation for propositional functions which allows for this great development and so makes it seem at least plausible that mathematics may be reduced to logic. Frege himself says in his preface that he thinks this is the most important novelty of the book.

In the second part of his *Begriffsschrift* Frege gives a set of logical rules and axioms which are complete in the sense of being sufficient for the demonstration of all the necessary truths of the restricted calculus of propositional functions, that is to say, of the calculus in which the universal quantifier 'all' is applicable only to letters marking gaps for the names of individuals, as distinct from letters marking gaps for the signs of qualities or relations. He thought, probably, that he had done more than this; but when he wrote there was as yet no established technique for proving the completeness or incompleteness of axiom sets, and it was not until 1930 and 1931 that Gödel proved, first, the completeness of Frege's axiom set for the restricted calculus of propositional functions and, second, the impossibility of ever providing a complete axiom set for the enlarged calculus, which covers the same ground as Cantor's theory of sets. We shall see the importance of these discoveries in a moment.

In the third part of the *Begriffsschrift* Frege shows, by way of illustration, how some important notions of the theory of order can be formulated in his symbolism. But this was to be only a preliminary to the big work of showing in detail how arithmetic can be derived from logic. No doubt he would have liked to go on to that immediately, but the reception of his first effort was discouraging, and he thought it best to try to present his main ideas in an informal fashion with a view, as he said, to making it seem at least probable that nothing is required in arithmetic but what is already granted in logic. This he did in his *Grundlagen der Arithmetik* (Foundations of Arithmetic) of 1884. The book is written in vigorous German without logical symbolism, and it contains lively criticisms of the views of contemporary mathematicians and philosophers, in particular of the formalists, who thought mathematical truth was somehow made by human conventions for the use of signs. It is probably the best known of Frege's writings, and it has recently been translated into English by Professor Austin. The central thesis is that a natural number can be defined without recourse to any notions except those of logic. I cannot give the details of the rather complicated definition here, but I must draw attention to the fact that it involves free use of the notion of a class or set. It is equivalent, in effect, to the definition of the cardinal number of a set as the set of all sets that can be put into one-one correspondence with the given set. This use of the notion of a set is important, because when Frege talked of reducing arithmetic to logic he always thought of logic as including Cantor's theory of sets. He made it clear, indeed, that he agreed with Cantor in thinking it possible to develop a theory of transfinite cardinals. Cantor, who was constantly under attack on this score, needed all the support he could get; but he was apparently too much harassed by criticism to recognize a friend when he found one, and he wrote an unfavourable review of Frege's work.

Although he had so far received no encouragement from anyone, Frege went on slowly with his grand project, and in 1893 he produced the first volume of his *Grundgesetze der Arithmetik* (Fundamental Laws of Arithmetic) which was intended to provide a rigorous proof of his thesis by means of his special symbolism. The work was done with great care, and in the course of it Frege elaborated a distinction between meaning and reference which has attracted a lot of attention in recent years, though it made no great stir at the time. The second volume appeared ten years later, that is, in 1903 ; but at the end there was a Postscript, written after the body of the work had been printed, in which Frege acknowledged sadly that a young Englishman, called Bertrand Russell, had just convinced him of the possibility of producing a contradiction within his system. This was the famous antinomy of the class of all classes that are not members of themselves. If this class is a member of itself, then it is not a member of itself; and if it is not, then it is. Even before that date Cantor himself had found an antinomy in his own theory of sets, and within a few years several more were discovered. From that time on, the chief interest of writers on the foundations of mathematics has been to determine what can be saved of the theory of sets. And since the discovery of Gödel in 1931, which I mentioned earlier, there has been a fairly widespread view among logicians that the theory of sets should not in any case be accounted part of logic. If we adopt that view, then clearly we must say that arithmetic cannot be reduced to logic. This is partly a question of what we choose to call logic, but it is important, because a big gulf has been discovered where Frege could see nothing but a difference of levels.

When he received Russell's letter, Frege realized that the trouble was due to his uncritical assumption of the existence of a class corresponding to each functional expression that might be constructed, and he made some suggestions for a reform of his system, but after 1903 he published very little more on the foundations of arithmetic, though there were vigorous debates during the last twenty-two years of his life. In 1908, for example, there appeared papers by Russell, Zermelo, and Brouwer which suggested three radically different ways of dealing with the antinomies. Things were moving fast, and to the younger thinkers it naturally seemed a waste of time to master an outmoded symbolism for the purpose of reading a work which the author himself had admitted to be defective. That is why until recently most of Frege's influence was exercised through Whitehead and Russell.

As might be expected, this influence is most obvious in the philosophy of mathematics and connected studies. I explained a moment ago why it now seems undesirable to talk of the reduction of arithmetic to logic, but I do not want to give you the impression that Frege's work was wasted. On the contrary, Gödel's theorem of 1931, which shows the impossibility of ever providing a complete axiom set for all mathematics, could not have been proved without the introduction of a strict logical symbolism like that of Frege. And since 1931 there have been other interesting discoveries in the theory of mathematical proof. Sometimes, people who are sceptical of the value of the study ask whether it has ever helped mathematicians to get results they could not have obtained otherwise. The answer to this question is 'Yes — but results of a rather queer kind, about mathematical systems'. For some relatively simple theories it has been possible to provide a decision procedure, that is to say, a rule of thumb which will enable us to determine in a finite number of steps whether a proposition formulated in the symbolism of the theory is true or false. But the most interesting cases are those in which it has been shown that there can be no decision procedure ; and one of these is the restricted calculus of propositional functions, that is, the logical system for which Frege provided the first complete axiom set. In other words, while we now know for certain that we have everything needed for the proof of any theorem in this system, we know also that, except in certain special cases, there can be no rule for the construction of proofs in the system. This is a very curious result, not so much because it is surprising that a system can be completely axiomatized and yet lack a decision procedure (though that *should* surprise people who hold a naïve conventionalist theory of logic and mathematics), but because it seems strange that we are able to *prove* these two properties of the system. The result is a long way, of course, from anything established by Frege himself, but I think he is entitled to some credit for the ingenuity of the reasoning which his work has made possible.

For the purpose of the present series of lectures it is more important, however, to notice the influence of mathematical philosophy on general philosophy during the present century. First, there was a revival of Leibniz's project for a perfect language, that is, a language which would mirror the structure of facts without distortion. However ill-conceived this project may be, it seemed natural enough to those who had just succeeded in producing a simple and elegant symbolism for logic. Admittedly neither Frege nor Russell was as hopeful as Leibniz, who had looked forward to a time when men of goodwill, finding themselves in disagreement, would pick up their pens and say *Calculemus* — 'Let us calculate' — because they knew that the source of their disagreement could be removed by strict attention to the rules of their scientific language. But Russell has often suggested that our philosophical difficulties arise from the imperfections of ordinary language; and at one time Wittgenstein said expressly that sentences could do their work only by mirroring the structure of facts. Secondly, it was often supposed that philosophical problems such as that about the status of material objects might be solved in the same way as problems about the status of numbers of higher type. Just as Cantor had suggested that a real number was an infinite set of rational numbers which would ordinarily be called successive approximations to its true value, so Russell suggested that a table might be an infinite set of sense-data and sensibilia which would ordinarily be called appearances of it. I do not think this is a good analogy; and when you have heard the other talks in this series, you may perhaps be inclined to say that the influence of mathematical philosophy on general philosophy has been unfortunate — though, I think you will agree that it has at least produced some interesting novelties.

39

However, that may be, I do not want to end this lecture by speaking of Frege as though he were important only for his influence, direct or indirect, good or bad, on other people. His works are still worth reading for their own sake; and unless our Universities and libraries are all destroyed by war, his achievement in setting out the first complete system of formal logic should be remembered by a few people for a few thousand years. As Humpty Dumpty said, 'There's glory for you'.

# LOGICAL ATOMISM:
## RUSSELL AND WITTGENSTEIN

A T the beginning of this century philosophy passed through one of those periods of rapid development which historians of ideas call revolutions. The centre of the new movement was England, and, more particularly, Cambridge, and its leaders were Moore, Russell, and Wittgenstein. Perhaps it is unfortunate that we find it natural to picture such rapid changes as revolutions. For this political analogy sometimes leads people to exaggerate the extent of the break with the past. Certainly this kind of presentation of the recent history of philosophy has had this effect. People see no connection between the type of philosophy which is now dominant in England and the Idealism of the second half of the nineteenth century. But the connection exists, and it deserves to be described. Russell, for instance, is an empiricist, and he stands in the direct line of descent from Locke and Hume : but, in spite of this, he owes much to the idealists whose philosophy stems from Kant. The very titles 'empiricist' and 'idealist' encourage over-simplification. German idealism is said to have effected a revolution in English thought in the first half of the nineteenth century, a revolution which did not entirely eliminate its rivals, but established its ascendancy until the end of the century, when empiricism staged a rather more successful counter-revolution. Not that this picture is actually false : but it leaves out qualifications of very great interest.

Perhaps some of these qualifications can be collected from a comparison of Russell's philosophy with the philosophy of F. H. Bradley. Bradley, as Mr. Wollheim pointed out in the first lecture in this series, is better understood through his hostilities than through his allegiances. He was bitterly hostile to the contemporary representatives of the empiricist tradition, both because of the general nature of their conclusions and because he thought that their method was psychological. For they operated with ideas rather than with judgements or propositions, and this, Bradley thought, was a mistake. Now the empiricists' neglect of judgements had always been the main target of idealist criticism : it was really the deepest difference between Kant and Hume. What Russell did was to absorb this part of the idealist tradition, and put it at the service of empiricism. For the new philosophy is really an empiricism based on judgements or propositions, instead of being based on ideas. And this was an important advance, since propositions are complete units of thought, whereas ideas, like terms or separate words, are incomplete fragments. I do not mean to suggest that Russell alone was responsible for the development of this new kind of empiricism : Moore and Wittgenstein made their own distinctive contributions to it. Nor do I mean to suggest that the practice of studying whole propositions rather than the separate terms out of which they are formed is entirely derived from the idealists : it is also derived from other sources, the most important of which is the work of Frege. But the debt to idealism needs emphasizing because it is too often forgotten.

It is time that I defined my subject more closely. In general, it is the rapid development of philosophy at the beginning of this century ; but, more particularly, it is the philosophical movement which Russell called Logical Atomism. The effect of narrowing my subject in this way is to concentrate attention on Russell and Wittgenstein rather than on Moore. For, though some of the ideas of this movement influenced Moore's early work, he stood rather aloof, on the edge of it : whereas Russell and Wittgenstein were in the centre of it. Not that one can describe Russell and Wittgenstein as logical atomists, and leave it at that. This would be misleading. Russell's work spans sixty years, and Wittgenstein's nearly forty years. Russell gradually evolved the leading ideas of logical atomism in the first two decades of this century, and then, in his later works, has repudiated some of them, but not all of them. Wittgenstein became a pupil of Russell in the second decade of the century, accepted these ideas, modified them and developed them in a deeper way than Russell, and in the end criticized and rejected them more thoroughly and comprehensively than Russell has ever done. But I shall not discuss the later stages of the thought of these two philosophers. The period with which I am concerned is 1900 to 1920, the subject logical atomism and the scene Cambridge.

The name 'Logical Atomism' was invented by

Russell, the author of the theory, and it is an entirely appropriate name, which really tells us something about the character of the theory. It brings out the relationship with Hume, who was also a kind of philosophical atomist. For Hume tried to explain everything in terms of the impressions and ideas, which are, according to him, the sole contents of human minds. The word 'atomism' is, of course, a metaphor: just as the scientist was supposed to go on dividing objects until he reached their ultimate, indivisible parts, so the philosopher's task was conceived as a kind of analysis of thought into its ultimate, simple elements. But, whereas Hume believed that philosophers ought to practise psychological analysis of ideas, Russell maintained that the analysis should deal with propositions, and so Russell qualified his kind of atomism as logical. So, you see, on this point Russell agreed with Bradley rather than with Hume: for, as Mr. Wollheim pointed out, Bradley too maintained that philosophers should study logic, and avoid psychology. But after this point of agreement Russell and Bradley diverged widely. Russell opened the lectures on logical atomism which he gave in 1918 by rejecting the idealist view that analysis must lead to distortion. He said: 'One is often told that the process of analysis is falsification, and that when you analyse any given concrete whole you falsify it, and that the results of analysis are not true. I do not think that is a right view.' You will remember that Bradley had said that 'It is a very common and ruinous superstition to suppose that analysis is no alteration'.

Russell did not produce detailed arguments to

support his view that analysis need not distort: he thought that it would be sufficiently established if his own programme of logical analysis could be carried out successfully. But what are the criteria of success? This question takes us to the very centre of the new movement: so let me answer it by quoting from Russell's essay entitled 'Logic as the Essence of Philosophy', which appeared in 1914. He said there that philosophers should 'give an account of the world of science and daily life'; but that many philosophers proved to be incapable of giving any such account 'because they were less anxious to understand the world of science and daily life than to convict it of unreality in the interests of a supra-sensible real world'. You see Russell's idea. If only we can succeed in understanding the way we talk and think about the ordinary world, we shall not be led to reject it in favour of another world behind it. In fact, he was being a little unfair to his opponents: as Mr. Wollheim pointed out, philosophers like Bradley do not actually reject our everyday beliefs about the world; they only say that in the end they are not intellectually satisfying, and that ultimately Reality cannot be like this. So perhaps Russell's point ought to have been expressed slightly differently, in the following way: If we succeeded in understanding our everyday beliefs we should find that they are, after all, intellectually satisfying; and this understanding can be reached only by analysis.

This programme may seem rather flat and pedestrian. Philosophers are no longer to produce systems of metaphysics, which are works of high

imaginative reason : instead they must try to describe
human thinking as it actually is, and to understand
it. Because this undertaking is in the spirit of the
age, people are so accustomed to reacting against it
that they do not pause to reflect that understanding
is neither dull nor easy. However, as we shall see,
logical atomism did not fulfil this undertaking. It
was Moore, the originator of the programme of
analysis, who really remained faithful to it, always
trying to understand the true nature of our thinking,
and never seeing patterns where they do not exist.
Moore's penetration and pertinacity are truly
Socratic, and no doubt they explain his aloofness
from logical atomism. For what Russell and Wittgenstein did in this period was to glimpse traces of
a pattern in our experience, and then, taking their
eyes off the facts, to develop this pattern far beyond
what is warranted by the facts. They had fixed
their eyes on logic ; for the recent advances in logic
and the foundations of mathematics which Mr.
Kneale described in the previous lecture in this
series encouraged them to hope that perhaps the
same kind of thing might be achieved in other
fields besides logic and mathematics. Perhaps even
ordinary empirical concepts might be reduced by
means of definitions to a few simple elements. But
though logic provided the model, aesthetic considerations also played a part. For the logical
atomists, like other metaphysicians, were seeking
clarity and order, and where they failed to discover
clarity and order, they invented them.

It may seem rather implausible to characterize
logical atomism as a metaphysical theory. For it is a

theory put forward by empiricists, and empiricists are notoriously anti-metaphysical. But we must not be misled by the way in which empiricists publicly denounce metaphysics. Such denunciations certainly reflect their intentions, but, in spite of these intentions, many empiricists are philosophical visionaries, just like metaphysicians. This can be verified by an examination of logical atomism, which is the result of a certain kind of philosophical vision. And it is worth verifying, since the belief that empiricists can never be metaphysicians is a strong contemporary delusion about the history of ideas.

Russell and Bradley assumed that, if you want to understand thought you must examine language, since it is in language that thought finds its expression. This common assumption naturally led them both to think that the proper study of philosophers is logic. What is more difficult to understand is the point on which Russell diverged from Bradley, *i.e.* his atomism. Hume's psychological atomism is quite plausible: we can easily be led to accept the theory that all complex ideas are built up out of simple ideas. But logical atomism is perhaps less easy to understand. Let us begin with propositions, since this is the point at which Russell begins his exposition of the theory. Propositions state facts, and are expressed by sentences: they are, roughly, what we ordinarily call statements. But how can they be divided into the atoms out of which they are built up? Well, take for example the statement that this thing in front of me — I mean this fountain-pen — is black. Bradley maintained that anyone who makes such a statement is illicitly dividing the thing from its quality, blackness, and that the copula, the word 'is', fails to mend the breach. As Mr. Wollheim pointed out, the analogy here is with those experiences of the artist in which there is diversity without separateness. Russell's rejoinder to this was that the two elements which are involved in this statement, the thing and its blackness, just fit together in an absolutely natural way. Certainly we can consider each of them separately, and find a word for each of them; but to do this is not to shatter or distort our experience; and so, when we ascribe blackness to the thing, we are not giving the copula an impossible task, the task of restoring a unity which can never be restored.

Notice how cool, sensible, and realistic this rejoinder is, altogether in the spirit of the new movement. Not that Russell decries the experience of the artist: he is only asking us not to condemn our more everyday experiences because they do not come up to this high standard. And this plea for toleration is surely right. For the final outcome of Bradley's theory would be silence: language would always seem to be too coarse and rough to catch reality in its net without damaging it; so every statement would need endless qualification, and nothing could ever be said. Bradley was judging and condemning language by an unattainable standard.

When a philosophical thesis is true, it often has a kind of obviousness and inevitability which make it seem unimportant. So, perhaps, it is worth emphasizing the importance of Russell's defence of ordinary statements. Russell's point is that qualities

and things fit together naturally: and he also says
that this is true of relations and things. In both
cases the logical fit is perfect, and this fact is brought
out by Russell's logical notation, in which the
predicate is placed next to the subject, and the
copula simply drops out. You might say that
Russell regards qualities and relations as objects;
not as particular things, of course, but as general
objects. This treatment of qualities and relations
which was in any way like Frege's treatment of
them, made it possible to rebut some of the more
paradoxical views of the idealists. For one of
Bradley's reasons for condemning the statement that
this thing is black had been that it absurdly tries to
*identify* the thing with blackness. Now this argument,
which is characteristic of idealist logic, treats blackness as a particular thing, and not as a general
object: consequently it makes it seem that the verb
'is' in this statement must be the 'is' of identity and
not the copula; and this, of course, is absurd, for
the fountain-pen cannot be identified with blackness.
But one escape from this paradox is to say that
blackness is a general object, which is not identified
with the thing, but only ascribed to it; and Russell
used this way of escape. However, it is not the
only way of escape.

You see how the theory of logical atomism
develops. You begin with statements, subject them
to analysis and find that they are built up out of
parts. Now some of these parts name objects in the
world. Clearly the copula does not name an object,
but many other words do. And objects are of
two kinds: first there are particular things; and

49

secondly there are qualities and relations, which are general objects. So we are to picture the world as an aggregate of separable things, qualities and relations, which are, as it were, particles. The justification of this picture is that, if you did not know what these particles were like, you would never be able to understand statements in which their names occurred. And the particles must be separable from one another; for, if you could not get to know some of them separately, you could never begin to get to know any of them. It would be like that irritating game in which you are given a heap of small pieces of ivory and you have to detach one piece from the heap without moving any of the other pieces; but they are all so twisted and hooked that this is almost impossible. But this is not an exact analogy: for, if the idealists were right, all separation and logical analysis would be quite impossible.

So far I have talked about analysis and particles, but I have said very little about atoms. Now the word 'atom' means 'indivisible particle', and it remains to be shown how Russell and Wittgenstein came to believe that there must be indivisible logical particles; and indeed, what sense can be attached to the notion of logical indivisibility. It is at this point that the theory ceases to be realistic and becomes metaphysical. For from now on, instead of describing the ways in which we actually think and speak, it claims to see a pattern which is not really there, or rather is not there in its entirety. For there actually are traces of the pattern which Russell and Wittgenstein said that they saw, but the traces are not very extensive. What they claimed was that when the pattern disappears, it is really there all the time, submerged by irrelevant detail.

There really is some plausibility in the thesis that some general objects are atomic; it is when the theory is extended to particular things that it ceases to be plausible. Let us first consider general objects; for instance, qualities. Some qualities are complex, and it is impossible to learn the meanings of the adjectives which name them, unless one already knows the meanings of other less complex words. This is true of the quality deciduousness, which is related in this way to foliage and falling: the idealists called this kind of relation 'internal', and it was Frege who first explained clearly how it depends on a definition. Now, if we think about such complex qualities, it seems that there must also be simple qualities, like blackness, which do not need to be introduced by definitions involving other qualities. It seems that this must be so, since, otherwise, we should never be able to begin to learn the meanings of any general words. This was Hume's line of thought. What Russell did was to present it logically instead of psychologically, and he called the simple qualities atomic. So here we have one kind of logical atom.

Now, so far, the theory obviously has much to commend it. For we certainly couldn't teach anyone the meanings of all general words just by referring him to other general words, because this method of instruction would be circular. However, the theory contains an exaggeration, since it suggests that atomic qualities are absolutely independent of one another; and, as Wittgenstein points out in the *Tractatus*, this is not true of any qualities that we know. You see what has happened. The reaction against the idealists has gone too far. Certainly we should reject their notion that everything is logically connected with everything: but it does not follow that some things are not logically connected with anything. However, the theory has some plausibility when it is applied to general objects. When it is applied to particular things it ceases to be plausible.

Let us see what the theory says about particular things. The example which I took was the statement that this fountain-pen is black. When I say this you know that I am referring to the fountain-pen in my hand. You know this from the context in which I make the statement. Now Bradley tried to secure this uniqueness of reference without appealing to the context. Well, the logical atomists tried to do this too, but they tried to do it in a very different way. Bradley suggested that all we can do is to add more and more general descriptions of the thing, *e.g.* that it is black, hollow, slender, etc.; but even then, he said, we shall never secure uniqueness of reference; for however many descriptions we apply to it, it is still possible that there is another thing exactly like it, satisfying all these descriptions. Russell, on the other hand, moved in the opposite direction: he said that, if we ask for the subject of all these descriptions, we shall find that it is what he calls a 'particular' and that this particular just is uniquely named by what he called a 'logically proper name'. Thus Russell thought that he could achieve uniqueness of reference by moving in the direction of greater and greater simplicity until he reached particulars : while Bradley moved in the direction of greater and greater complexity, towards the Absolute, but knew that by doing so he would never succeed in securing uniqueness of reference. Russell's particulars are, of course, the other kind of logical atom.

Notice that all this rests on the assumption that the meaning of a word is the thing designated by it. Once this is granted, then, since Russell thought that we must be able to learn the meanings of some names of things separately and in complete isolation from everything else, it follows that there must be absolutely simple particulars. Russell's ideal was really a sort of context-free language, like scientific language, only containing particular statements instead of the general statements that one finds in the text-books of science. And this ideal language was somehow thought to lie beneath ordinary language. For particulars are not ordinary things like this fountain-pen, since ordinary things are complex. If I refer to this thing as a fountain-pen, somebody might ask what is this thing which is a fountain-pen ; and the logical atomists thought that, if you went on stripping off descriptions in this way, you would eventually reach absolutely simple particulars, which would be the true subjects of all discourse. Wittgenstein, in the *Tractatus*, makes it clear that this doctrine is a new version of the old theory of individual substances. And it is vulnerable to the same objection as the old theory. If a philosopher begins by saying that things are, from a logical point of view, like Chinese boxes, then he really must carry this theory through to the end : he should not lose his nerve and say that inside the last box there must be something which, unlike the boxes, is solid and indivisible, something which cannot be described but only named, an individual substance. Now this objection did not always convince philosophers who supported the old theory of individual substances. But, when it is turned against Wittgenstein's version of the theory, I think it is possible to make it convincing. For, if we ask what is this thing which is a fountain-pen, and if we go on stripping off its descriptions in this way, it is surely quite clear that the subject of our last statement will not name any hidden centre of the kind which the logical atomists called a particular. They thought that there must be such particulars only because they assumed that the subjects of all these statements, including the last one, must name separate things. But there are good reasons for thinking that this assumption is mistaken.

Many of these reasons are set out in Wittgenstein's second book, written after he had changed his mind on this topic. But I shall not discuss them here, since they belong to a later stage in the development of analytical philosophy. In any case it was not my intention to describe the development of the ideas of any single philosopher : I have, for instance said nothing about the differences between Russell's and Wittgenstein's versions of logical atomism. I have only tried to present the main features of the theory, which is a very strange early result of logical analysis. Incidentally, I have also tried to explain how the school of analytic philosophy is related to its pre-decessors. For it is not the thunderbolt that it is popularly supposed to be, but is connected in many ways with earlier schools of philosophy. Its closest affinity is with the philosophy of Locke and Hume, but it is also indebted to the idealists, and to the new school of logicians. Its aim is to understand the ways in which we think, and this is why logical atomism is such a strange result for it to reach. For logical atomism is scarcely less unrealistic than Bradley's monism. True, it stands at the opposite pole from monism: it takes everything separately, whereas monism takes everything together. But both theories are of the same general type: both operate with the same set of philosophical concepts — object, particle, division, and synthesis — and, although they give these concepts a logical interpretation, nevertheless they say things which are fully intelligible only if we visualize them in physical terms. Almost all metaphysical theories rely on this device. I suppose Plato was the first philosopher to exploit it thoroughly. Perhaps it is the only convincing way of speaking about metaphysical reality. But the philosophers who used it did not adopt it deliberately or artificially. It seems an artificial device only to those who have no tendency to metaphysics. To the metaphysician, whose intellect and imagination work together, it is the most natural thing in the world: he cannot help visualizing things in this way, and he is convinced that the patterns which he sees are really there. If this were not so, it would be impossible to explain how Russell, when he set out to explain the world of science and daily life, produced instead a theory which is, in the deepest sense, Platonic.

# G. E. MOORE: ANALYSIS, COMMON
# USAGE, AND COMMON SENSE

I N 1903 there appeared in the journal *Mind* an
article by G. E. Moore of Cambridge called 'The
Refutation of Idealism'.[1]  An attempt he made
some years later to state briefly his own position was
called, by contrast, 'A Defence of Common Sense'.[2]
Why did common sense need defending? What has
it to do with philosophy?

The idealist philosopher F. H. Bradley of Oxford,
in his book *Appearance and Reality* published ten years
before, had reasserted, with some force of rhetoric
and splendid writing, the vast claim of metaphysics
to prove 'striking and important' conclusions about
the nature of the-universe-as-a-whole, 'Reality'.
'We may agree perhaps', he wrote, 'to understand
by metaphysics the effort to comprehend the universe
not simply piecemeal or by fragments, but somehow
as-a-whole.'[3]  The proofs started from an attempt
to show that familiar facts and things are not as
common sense takes them to be; are not real; are,
as Bradley put it, mere 'Appearance'.  Here, then, is
one way in which it can be important in philosophy
to offer a defence of common sense; important for
metaphysics and not merely for analytic philosophy.

[1] Reprinted in *Philosophical Studies*, 1922.
[2] In *Contemporary British Philosophy*, ed. J. H. Muirhead, 1925.
[3] *Appearance and Reality*.

Bradley's conceptions of 'reality', 'existence', and 'appearance', and their relation to 'what ordinary people would mean' by these words, were investigated much later by Moore in an article of 1917 called 'The Conception of Reality'. The claim he tried there to resist is one of the most persistent, disturbing, and exciting in metaphysics, the claim that Time is not real.

But the most important hope and claim of metaphysical philosophers has nearly always been to discover in the ultimate nature of reality some source of ethics, some warrant for rules about how we are to behave towards one another. In pursuing this hope Bradley was in company with men so wide apart as Plato and Hume, though Hume had explicitly tried to reject it. Moore would not have it. In his book *Principia Ethica*, published in 1903, and, above all, in the chapter called 'Metaphysical Ethics', he tried to show that this imposing claim often involved a special case of a fallacy of confusion, to which he gave a name, now well known, 'the naturalistic fallacy'.

Yet in this very chapter Moore made it plain that he was far from being in all matters out of sympathy with metaphysics. 'Metaphysicians', he wrote, 'have recognised and insisted that there are, or may be, objects of knowledge which we cannot *perceive*; and in recognising the possibility of these as a subject for investigation, they have, it may be admitted, done a service to mankind',[1] and similarly, in 'The Refutation of Idealism', 'I consider it to be the main service of the philosophic school to which

[1] p. 111.

modern Idealists belong that they have insisted on distinguishing 'sensation' and 'thought', and on emphasizing the importance of thought. Against Empiricism, they have maintained the true view.'[1]

It will be evident from these remarks that Moore was not eager to show everything to be a matter of what can be perceived, or sensed; that he was no positivist. Indeed, in ethics, he tried hard to show that the fundamental word 'good' is sometimes used to stand for a quality which *cannot* come under empirical observation, which is, as he put it, 'not a *natural* quality'.[2]

But he *was* an 'analyst'. 'It appears to me', he wrote, 'that in Ethics, as in all other philosophical studies, the difficulties and disagreements, of which its history is full, are mainly due to a very simple cause: namely to the attempt to answer questions, without first discovering precisely what question it is which you desire to answer'; often 'what moral philosophers have before their minds is not one question but *several*', what they need to do is 'the work of *analysis* and *distinction*', which, however, is often very difficult.[3]

To give an example: 'Modern idealism', said Moore, 'if it asserts any general conclusion about the universe at all, asserts that it is *spiritual*'; the assertion is deceptively simple, and will be found on analysis to be complicated and imprecise. When the idealist philosopher declares that it is '*spiritual*, he means to include in that term quite a *large* number of different properties'; that it is, for

[1] p. 7    [2] *Principia Ethica*, p. 39.
[3] First paragraph of the Preface to *Principia Ethica*.

example, 'intelligent, that it is purposeful, that it is not mechanical',[1] perhaps indeed that 'the *whole* universe possesses *all* the qualities the possession of which is held to make us so superior to things which seem to be inanimate'.[2]

Moore emphasized this because he thought that 'we are apt to overlook the *number* of *different* propositions which the idealist must prove', 'we are apt to forget what a *vast* number of arguments this interesting and important question must involve; we are apt to assume that if *one or two* points be made on either side, the whole case is won'.[3] By contrast, the first step in a proper procedure is to discriminate within the one deceptively simple formula a number of distinct, separate questions. The next is to select one key question on which to begin the intensive examination.

Here is a further example from the start of *Principia Ethica*: 'This, then, is our first question: What is good? . . . But this is a question which may have many meanings'.[4] And again, from *The Refutation of Idealism*; referring to Berkeley's question whether to exist is to be perceived, he said, 'But now: Is *esse percipi*? There are *three very ambiguous* terms in this proposition. . . .'[5] Yet the single proposition 'Esse is percipi' is 'a necessary and *essential* step in all Idealistic arguments'.[6] And again, 'the question, how "good" is to be defined, is *the most fundamental* question in all Ethics'.[7]

Moore was meticulous to mark how limited and restricted were his aims. He had no programme.

[1] *Philosophical Studies*, p. 1.  [2] p. 2.  [3] p. 2.
[4] p. 3.  [5] p. 7.  [6] p. 3.  [7] *Principia Ethica*, p. 5.

'Even if I prove my point', he wrote, 'I shall have proved nothing about the Universe in general. The subject of this paper is (I am afraid) quite uninteresting.'[1] Or again, in discussing Ethics, 'if I am asked "How is good to be defined?" my answer is that it cannot be defined, and that is all I have to say about it, disappointing though this answer may appear'.[2] They were small gains, he announced; but gains and definite.

But all the same, they had, he thought, consequences of 'the very last importance'.[3] In Ethics, for example, he asserted, 'if I am right nobody can foist on us [as some Utilitarians have done], such an *axiom* as that "Pleasure is the only good"';[4] and in metaphysics 'it will follow that, unless new reasons never urged hitherto can be found [all the most striking results] of philosophy have as little claim to assent as the most superstitious beliefs of the most ignorant savages'.[1] The bearing of his arguments was not directly upon the matters themselves, but 'upon the question *what we have reason to believe* in these most interesting matters'.[5]

Moore did not suggest (as positivists have done since) that metaphysics was nonsense, but rather that its claims, though deceptively simple and straightforward, were in fact complicated and confused, immoderate, and based on 'one or two'[6] arguments only, too flimsy altogether for their superstructure.

And although he raised questions of 'ambiguity' and 'meaning', he was anxious to assure his readers

---

[1] *Philosophical Studies*, p. 4.    [2] *Principia Ethica*, p. 6.
[3] p. 6.    [4] p. 7.
[5] *Philosophical Studies*, p. 5.    [6] p. 2.

that his questions were not primarily about usage of words : 'my business is not with . . . proper usage, as established by custom',[1] for 'verbal questions are properly left to the writers of dictionaries and other persons interested in literature; philosophy has no concern with them'.[2] 'What I want to discover', he said, 'is the nature of a certain object or idea.'[3]

One purpose of Moore's care about words was to try to make the reader notice for the first time what was already there, before his mind; of one case he wrote that 'where we try to introspect, a certain element is as if it were diaphanous. Yet it *can* be distinguished, if we look attentively enough, and if we know that there is something to look for. My main object here has been to try to *make* the reader *see* it.'[4] Similarly, in *Principia Ethica*, 'whoever will attentively consider with himself *what is actually before his mind when* he asks the question can *easily come to recognize* that in each case he has *before his mind* not one object but two'.[5]

In both metaphysics and ethics, Moore thought certain vast conclusions had come to exert on many of us a fascination which could be broken only if we dissected and scrutinized with a new standard of care certain crucial stages in our reasoning. If we attended to what was actually before our mind at those stages something diaphanous could be made discernible, or else two things at first confused could be made distinct. By this the spell would be broken, and our minds set free to ask afresh 'what there is?' and 'what there is that is good?' *Principia Ethica* is

[1] *Principia Ethica*, p. 6.    [2] p. 2.    [3] p. 6.
[4] *Philosophical Studies*, p. 25.    [5] p. 16.

not, he pointed out, a book on morals (except for a tentative final chapter) ; it is a *preparation* for reaching conclusions in morals, by trying 'to discover the principles of moral reasoning'.[1]

(He did, however, claim that such 'conclusions' in morals as he had 'attempted to present'[2] would be found 'very different from any which have commonly been advocated by philosophers' !)[1]

Moore introduced another important critical device, that of bringing home to his reader the force of some abstract term by familiar concrete substitutes. On the claim that 'the universe is spiritual', his opening remark was this: 'Chairs and tables, and mountains *seem* to be very different from us'; but when the whole universe is declared to be spiritual, it is certainly meant to assert that *they* are far more like *us* than we think'.[3] And in resisting Bradley's claim that 'Time is unreal' Moore noted that 'of course, Time with a big T seems to be a highly abstract kind of entity',[4] and that to define *exactly* what can be meant by 'Time is unreal' does seem to offer difficulties. But, he advised, try translating it into the concrete. You will find yourself thinking: 'if "Time is unreal", then plainly nothing ever happens *before* or *after* anything else; it is never true that anything is *past*; never true that anything will happen in the *future*; never true that anything is happening *now*, and so on'.[5] Moore did not start to deal systematically with Bradley's

[1] p. ix.

[2] pp. 188-9, 'personal affection, and the appreciation of what is beautiful, are good in themselves'. 'They include *all* the greatest goods.'

[3] *Philosophical Studies*, p. 1.     [4] p. 209.     [5] p. 210.

paradox until he had sharpened the paradox, bringing it home to his reader in these immediate terms.

Again, ask yourself, he advised, when philosophers
have voiced doubt of the existence of the External
World, have they intended *me* to doubt that here *I*
hold up *my* hand in front of *me*.[1]

Doubt of the existence or reality of an external
world has not been peculiar to those philosophers
whom we primarily think of as speculative or metaphysical. For example, Bertrand Russell, in his book
*Our Knowledge of the External World*, held that 'the
*common-sense* belief in fairly permanent bodies —
tables, chairs, mountains, is a piece of audacious
*metaphysical* theorizing',[2] and in *The Problems of
Philosophy*, that though 'it seems to me that I am
sitting in a chair, at a table of a certain shape, on
which I see sheets of paper and writing', yet 'all
this may reasonably be doubted, and all of it requires
much careful discussion before we can be sure that
we have stated it in a form that is *wholly* true'.[3]

Moore's *Defence of Common Sense* opened with a
comprehensive list of just such truisms, together with
a blunt denial that they were always 'open to
reasonable doubt', and a blunt assertion that '*every-
one* of them I *know* to be true'. And, he added, true,
not just in some emended form, or in some special
usage of the words employed; he meant by each
of them precisely what every reader, in reading them,
will have understood him to mean, *i.e.* what they
are *ordinarily* understood to express. Furthermore,
such an expression as 'The earth has existed for

[1] In *Proof of an External World.*
[2] p. 167.          [3] pp. 10-11.

many years past' is *the very type* of an *unambiguous* expression, the meaning of which *we all* understand.[1]

Moore did not rest content with bare denial and assertion : he gave arguments, as, for example, that those who claim not to know such truisms 'betray' that they do know them by '*alluding to* the existence of other philosophers',[2] and even by 'alluding to the existence of the human race' in using the pronoun 'we'.[2] And he noted it as a strange fact that people do frequently hold sincerely, as part of their philosophical creed, beliefs inconsistent with what they themselves *know* to be true.[2]

It will be seen that in this paper of 1925, Moore now had come to show interest in and respect for how a phrase is '*ordinarily* understood', 'the meaning *we all* understand', in marked contrast to his pronouncement in 1903, 'my business is *not* with proper usage, as established by custom'.[3]

Already by 1917 in *The Conception of Reality* he had shown that he was becoming aware of one important reason for this respect. In discussing Bradley's claim that Time is unreal, he had noted a danger inherent in giving to a simple common phrase like this any special, as it were *technical*, meaning : the danger, namely, of slipping unawares from the special back to the ordinary ; that is, of an unnoticed change, or even duplicity, of meaning, the very curse which analytic discrimination had originally been brought in to cure. 'What I cannot help thinking', he wrote, 'is that, even if Mr. Bradley is using the words "Time is unreal" in a *highly unusual and special* sense,

[1] *A Defence of Common Sense*, p. 198.      [2] p. 203.
[3] *Principia Ethica*, p. 6.

he does mean *as well* what ordinary people would mean' by those words.[1]  And Moore hinted that it is just this two-faced character which fits such formulae to play their role in starting metaphysics. Familiar enough in style to make their sceptical impact on common sense, they *can* yet be defended as altogether other, special, technical, and aseptic in their significance.  Yet metaphysics when aseptic is apt to be also insipid.

Precise dissection of principles of reasoning in morals had exposed some principles which might be used, not merely in the manner of Descartes to re-establish what had been, but to present something 'very different'.  But, by contrast, in metaphysics a similar dissection of principles of reasoning had shown none in terms of which anything much of a metaphysical kind could be presented, new or even old.  Did it leave anything of some other kind to be presented ?

Not worried as earlier philosophers had been about whether he knew the truisms of common sense, or about alleged defects in them, Moore wrote : 'I am not at all sceptical as to the *truth* of such propositions ;  but I *am very* sceptical as to what . . . the correct *analysis* of them is', 'no philosopher hitherto has succeeded in suggesting an analysis of them, as regards certain important points, that comes anywhere near to being certainly true'.[2]

This should *not* be summarized in the slogan 'Philosophy is analysis' ;  Moore did not say that 'synthesis' is ruled out as senseless or too old fashioned.  But 'unless new reasons, never hitherto

[1] *Philosophical Studies*, p. 208.
[2] *A Defence of Common Sense*, p. 216.

urged could be found',[1] no one could get on with 'synthesis' and certainly Moore could not. Moore's own interest and powers were to be centred on examining with delicate discrimination what had nearly always been regarded as too commonplace or defective to give rise to wonder or to be worthy of care. 'We are all', he claimed, 'in this *strange* position; that we do know many things . . . and yet we do not know *how* we know them.'[2]

It may not seem much to write out a list of truisms, and champion them as being both wholly true and adequately expressed. It does seem 'quite uninteresting'; but it has had effects 'of the very last importance'.

Statements formulated in what are often called 'technical' terms are protected from criticism by this very unfamiliarity. From it they can gain also an air of remote authority which discourages inquiry. Mathematics has always provided one paradigm by comparison with which, to some philosopher or other, our everyday language has appeared shockingly defective. Plato was such a one; Descartes another. In our century advances that had been made, not only in pure mathematics, but also in the applying of mathematics to what happens, could not but strike many as making the devices of common speech seem crude and therefore objectionable. And this old disadvantageous comparison was strengthened by there coming to be developed within a branch of philosophy itself, namely logic, examples of just such strict, precise, satisfyingly manageable systems. Add

[1] *Philosophical Studies*, p. 5.
[2] *Contemporary British Philosophy*, p. 208.

to all that, the striking success and growth of the sciences in this century, and the attendant prestige attaching to their ways and words, and you will see that there has come to be even more need than ever there was in the far-off simple times of Bradley for someone to stand firm for any merits the common tongue may possess. Moore has insisted over a long period that the common usage of the ordinary person (in which in any case much of any subject is conducted) is not to be *lightly* declared rough, vague, ambiguous, and so on. He has tried to show that many paradoxes are formulated in terms of common usage, and revisions of it proposed, *not* from a new insight into its crude defects, but from an old, continuing failure to work out exactly *what* it is. Once that is discriminated and displayed, it may in many cases appear that no paradox arises, or that no revision is needed.

In standing firm for this, Moore has needed what he has, the courage to seem naïve; and I hope 'it may be admitted that in this he has done a service to mankind'. We can admit *this*, even if we *do* think that Moore *has* been naïve and wrong; we have only to imagine how beneficial it must have been to metaphysical and logico-scientific philosophers to have to explain to Moore *just* where usage is defective, *just* what in the truism is not quite true.

Moore has been criticized as having made a fetish of ordinary usage, a scholasticism of it, treating it as sacrosanct. Yet his point has been not that it never should be altered or added to, but only that before doing either we should study to know what it is; and then often will not wish to alter or add.

THE REVOLUTION IN PHILOSOPHY

But we may. Moore has himself in his writings both given to some common words a highly specialized sense, and also for certain purposes introduced new words, as for example 'sense-datum'. But he has done so only where he thought he could show a need, and has tried always to give notice, and a full account, of the new use. His repeated meticulous and energetic attempts to explain exactly why he requires the word 'sense-datum' and exactly how it is to be used has long stood as a model of procedure, in no way diminished by the fact that it does not succeed.

Questions about perception have engaged his typical absorbed energy more, probably, than any others. Time after time he has worried at them and come back to try again, insisting on an accuracy and completeness which have set a new standard in philosophy. In the effort to specify with precision what he wants to say, he has written many passages of involved, repetitive sentences which some people find too much, and which indeed have no grace. But often they do serve their purpose as nothing else could.

In this involvement Moore's style differs markedly from that of Russell, who even on the most difficult topics is always simple, easy, and elegant, full of something new to say; but often too full of it to be precise, explicit, complete. Moore, valuing Russell's ideas, has spent much thought and care in trying to make clear and precise his *special* concepts, for example, that of 'propositional function', Russell's informal accounts of which have appeared to shock him, if only by their variety.

And nearly always Moore has achieved his aims — to be clear and precise — in direct, simple, con-

versational language, utterly free from pretence.
The tired-out words of the subject are not there;
he conveys not only his meaning but a sense of
intense, lively concentration and effort, and his own
stress of work. It is far from the splendid, uneasy,
loose, scornful rhetoric of Bradley.

But Moore has conveyed his thoughts as much by
speech as writing. Over a long period he was the life
of many of the gatherings of philosophers in Britain.
When Moore was to read a paper or take part in
discussion, one could be sure that things would *go*.

But Moore was, I think, at his very best in his
class at Cambridge. It is not easy to imagine how
lecturing could be done better than he did it. The
subject matter of each lecture had obviously been
originally worked out in thorough detail with effort
and care; and gone over again, each time, in the
days preceding the lecture to be altered and made
better. Moore would arrive for his lecture with his
head evidently full of the problem, and the air of
one in whose week this was a most important and
worth-while occasion. He would then, writing and
drawing on the board, and with only rare glances at
his abandoned manuscript, work out afresh what he
had already done on the problem, trying once more
to make it better as he went on. 'While he talked,
he was obviously thinking hard about the subject
he was talking of, and searching for the best way
of putting what he wanted to convey.' Those
present were not left out as mere spectators, but
would become caught up in his activity, and search
in their own minds for what it was that he wanted
to convey.

# THE VIENNA CIRCLE

THE philosophical movement which is known as Logical Positivism originated, as a movement, with the Vienna Circle. This was a group of philosophers and mathematicians which formed itself around Professor Moritz Schlick when he came, in the year 1922, to occupy a chair of philosophy at Vienna University. On the philosophical side its leading members, apart from Schlick himself, were Friedrich Waismann, Rudolf Carnap, Otto Neurath, Herbert Feigl, and Victor Kraft; on the mathematical side, Hans Hahn, Karl Menger, and Kurt Gödel. Ludwig Wittgenstein, who was still living near Vienna when the group was being formed, was never officially a member of it, but he maintained close personal relations with Schlick and Waismann, which still continued after he had gone to teach at Cambridge, and the group was very much influenced by his ideas. His famous *Logische-Philosophische Abhandlung*, a work which is better known by the title given to its English translation, *Tractatus Logico-Philosophicus*, appeared in 1921; and to a considerable extent it set the pattern which, at least in its early days, the Vienna Circle followed. It is worth noticing, however, that many of the views which came to be regarded as especially characteristic of logical positivism had already been advanced by Schlick in his book on the theory of knowledge, *Allgemeine Erkenntnislehre*, which was published in 1918.

From the beginning the members of the Circle met regularly to discuss philosophical problems among themselves, but it was not until 1929 that they, as it were, registered themselves as a philosophical party. In that year they organized a Congress in Prague to which they invited sympathizers from other countries, and they brought out a manifesto entitled *Die wissenschaftliche Weltauffassung der Wiener Kreis* (the Scientific Standpoint (literally world-conception) of the Vienna Circle). Written by Carnap, Neurath, and Hahn, it paid tribute to Schlick and gave a summary account of the main tenets which the members of the group then held in common. In 1930 they took over a journal called *Annalen der Philosophie*, renamed it *Erkenntnis*, and used it as the principal vehicle for the diffusion of their ideas. Its editors were Carnap and Hans Reichenbach, the leader of a similar though less important movement in Berlin. They also in the thirties brought out a series of monographs with the collective title of *Einheitswissenschaft* (Unified Science) and a series of books, edited by Schlick and by the philosopher of science, Philipp Frank, then, like Carnap, a professor at the German University of Prague. Contributors to this series were not limited to members of the Vienna Circle. One of the best books to appear in it, a work on the philosophy of science called *Logik der Forschung*, was written by Karl Popper, now a professor at the London School of Economics, who, though working in Vienna, did not belong to the Circle and was in some important ways an opponent of its views. Not, as we shall see, that those who were members of it by any means always agreed among themselves.

Throughout the period contact was maintained with philosophers of similar tendencies in other countries, notably Poland, England, Holland, and Scandinavia, and further congresses were held at Prague, Copenhagen, Paris, and Cambridge. But by 1938, the year of the Cambridge congress, the Vienna Circle had practically ceased to exist. Schlick himself was killed in 1936, shot on the steps of the University by a demented pupil, whose thesis on ethics he had refused to pass; Hahn had died in 1934; Carnap, Feigl, Menger, and Gödel had gone to Universities in the United States; Neurath, who was particularly suspect to the Austrian governments of the later thirties — he had been an active member of the revolutionary Spartacist movement in Munich after the first world war — had taken refuge in Holland, and Waismann in England. This break-up of the Circle was mainly due to political causes. Its ideas were unpalatable to the right-wing clerical governments of Dollfuss and Schuschnigg and even more so to the Nazis who succeeded them. The opinion which has been advanced by ignorant and irresponsible journalists that logical positivism is favourable to fascism was not shared by the Fascists themselves. An attempt was made, chiefly by Neurath, to keep the movement in being on an international scale. The title of *Erkenntnis* was changed to *The Journal of United Science* and its place of publication to The Hague. A series of brochures ambitiously entitled *The International Encyclopaedia of Unified Science* was brought out in America under Neurath's direction but with a preponderance of American contributors. Further congresses were planned. But the war intervened, and with Neurath's death in England a year or two later, the movement lost its central direction. At the present time Kraft has resumed his chair of philosophy in Vienna, Waismann is an influential figure at Oxford, and Carnap, Gödel, and Feigl in the United States. But the Vienna Circle, as a movement, is a thing of the past. So, in a way, is logical positivism. But many of its ideas live on.

The expression 'logical positivism' had obtained such very wide currency that its use, except among professional philosophers, has become somewhat indiscriminate. Anyone who pursues philosophical analysis, in any of its multifarious forms, is liable to find himself labelled as a logical positivist, however little he may subscribe to the doctrines of the Vienna Circle. Even in the Circle this appellation was not much favoured — they preferred to describe themselves in ways which more explicitly brought out their reverence for science — but there it had its point. For the position which they held was, in its main features, a blend of the nineteenth-century Viennese positivism of the physicist, Ernst Mach, and his disciples, with the logic of Frege and Russell. So far as their positivism went they were continuing an old philosophical tradition — it is remarkable how many of their most radical doctrines are already to be found in Hume. Their originality lay in their attempt to make it logically rigorous and in their use for the purpose of a developed and sophisticated logical technique.

The positivist flavour of their thought comes out most strongly in their hostility to metaphysics. Metaphysics, which they construed as covering such allegedly philosophical enterprises as the attempt to describe Reality as a whole, or to find the purpose of the Universe, or to reach beyond the everyday world to some supra-sensible spiritual order, was condemned by them not as being unduly speculative, or even as being false, but as being literally nonsensical. They reached this conclusion by the application of a criterion of meaning which is known as the verification principle. The precise formulation of this principle is a complicated matter : I am not sure that it has even yet been satisfactorily done. But, roughly stated, it lays it down that the meaning of a statement is determined by the way in which it can be verified, where its being verified consists in its being tested by empirical observation. Consequently, statements like those of metaphysics to the truth or falsehood of which no empirical observation could possibly be relevant, are ruled out as factually meaningless. The emphasis here is on the word 'factually'. It is not denied that language has other uses besides that of imparting factual information. Nor is it maintained that these other uses are unimportant, or that metaphysical statements may not serve them. They may, for example, express an interesting and challenging attitude to life. All that is claimed is that they are not capable of stating facts.

In Wittgenstein's *Tractatus*, where the exclusion of

metaphysics is effected very sharply, there is none the less a slight suggestion that the metaphysician may be grasping at truths which only the limitations of language prevent him from describing. Its famous last sentence, 'Wovon man nicht sprechen kann darüber muss man schweigen' — somewhat archaically rendered by the English translators as 'Whereof one cannot speak, thereof one must be silent', seems to imply that there *are* things that one cannot speak about. The Vienna Circle rejected this suggestion. When it comes to metaphysics, said Neurath, 'one must indeed be silent, but not *about* anything'. Or as the Cambridge philosopher, F. P. Ramsey, an enthusiastic but critical follower of Wittgenstein, put it : 'What we can't say we can't say, and we can't whistle it either'. A great deal of bad philosophy comes from people thinking that they can somehow whistle what they cannot say.

A favourite argument of those who wish to defend metaphysics against the logical positivists' attack is that the verification principle is itself not verifiable. And, of course, it is not ; it was not meant to be. It was put forward as a definition, not as an empirical statement of fact. But it is not an arbitrary definition. It purports to lay down the conditions which actually govern our acceptance, or indeed our understanding, of common sense and scientific statements, the statements which we take as describing the world 'in which we live and move and have our being'. This leaves it open to the metaphysician to reply that there may be other worlds besides the world of science and common sense, and that he makes it his business to explore them. But then the onus is on him to show by what criterion his statements are to be tested : until he does this we do not know how to take them. What he cannot do, and what he too often tries to do, is to have it both ways ; putting forward his assertions as though they were scientific hypotheses, but of greater profundity and generality than scientific hypotheses normally are, and then, when it is shown that they do not qualify for this at all, taking refuge in saying that he does not expect them to : he is entering them for quite a different race. But then we want some information about the conditions under which this different race is run. To be disqualified from one race is not automatically to enter for another.

Leaving metaphysics aside, there were two important kinds of statements which the acceptance of the verification principle made it difficult to treat as statements of fact : the *a priori* statements of logic and pure mathematics, and statements of value, whether moral or aesthetic. The view, which has been held, for example by John Stuart Mill, that truths of logic and mathematics are empirical generalizations, makes it impossible to account for their necessity. The Vienna Circle allowed that they were necessary, but only because they were true by definition. They were said to be tautologies, in Wittgenstein's somewhat special use of this term. This was not intended to imply that they were trivial. Logic and mathematics have, on this theory, the important function of making it clear to what our use of symbols commits us. That we use them as we do is a matter of convention ; but once these conventions are established we are bound by them, not morally but in the sense that the infraction of them is self-stultifying. *A priori* statements are not themselves descriptive of anything, but their use enables us to pass securely from one descriptive statement to another. Wittgenstein, like Eddington, applies to our conceptual system the simile of a fisherman's net. Logic and mathematics are concerned only with the structure of the net, and therefore only with the form of the fish. Their truths are certain because we do not admit the possibility of their being falsified. There is a strong echo of Kant in this position, though Kant's own view of mathematics was on the face of it very different; and indeed the analogies between Kant and Wittgenstein are surprisingly close.

In general, the Vienna Circle accepted the Frege-Russell-Whitehead thesis that mathematics can be reduced to logic, though Gödel's own remarkable discoveries in this field have shown that this reduction, if possible at all, is charged with greater difficulties than was once supposed. But their view of *a priori* statements did not depend on this identification. Even if it is technically impossible to transform mathematical into logical statements, the explanation of their necessity may be the same.

With regard to statements of value, the one thing which was excluded by the verification principle was the metaphysical view that they are descriptive of a realm of values, which somehow exists on its own independently of the natural world. But this leaves several other alternatives open. Thus Schlick, who wrote a book about ethics called *Fragen der Ethik*, treated ethical statements as empirical. He upheld a form of utilitarianism according to which the validity of moral judgements depended on certain facts about human happiness and the means by which it was to be attained. The view which has come to be associated with logical positivism in this country, though it is not especially characteristic of the Vienna Circle, is that statements of value are emotive: they are not descriptive of anything, whether natural or non-natural; they express the speaker's feelings, or define his attitude. Consequently, they are neither true nor false, any more than commands are either true or false, though reasons can be given for them. This thesis has aroused considerable opposition, partly owing to the crudity of certain early formulations of it. It has been thought, quite mistakenly, that the seriousness of morals and aesthetics was somehow being impugned. In fact, it came to little more than development of the perfectly respectable logical point that normative statements are not derivable from descriptive statements or, as Hume put it, that you cannot deduce 'ought' from 'is'. Laying down a standard is not reporting a fact: but it is none the worse for that.

A corollary of this view is that it is not especially the business of the philosopher to make value judgements, to tell people how they ought to live. He is free to make value judgements, like anybody else, but he is not professionally entitled to a special hearing. It is not his particular province. But what then is his province? It is science that gives us our knowledge of the world; there is not, there cannot be, a philosophical brand of knowledge which would compete with science in this field. But where in that case does the philosopher come in? One thing he can do, of course, is to act as a sort of intellectual policeman, seeing that nobody trespasses into metaphysics. In the *Tractatus*, Wittgenstein seemed to think that this was all that he could do, though this opinion is in some degree belied by his own later work. 'The right method of philosophy', he said, 'would be this.' To say nothing except what can be said, *i.e.* the propositions of natural science, *i.e.* something that has nothing to do with philosophy : and then always, when someone else wished to say something metaphysical to demonstrate to him that he had given no meaning to certain signs in his propositions. This method would be unsatisfying to the other — he would not have the feeling that we were teaching him philosophy — but it would be the only strictly correct method.' The Vienna Circle, however, were not content with quite so negative a conception of philosophy as this. They thought that the philosopher still had a useful function to perform in analysing and clarifying the concepts which figure in the everyday, and also in the scientific use of language, but chiefly in the scientific use, as this was held to be the more important. Philosophy was to become the logic of science. In a sense, philosophy was to merge with science. There would not be a set of philosophical statements embedded among the scientific ones, but the scientific statements themselves would be refined by logical analysis. As Schlick put it, here echoing Wittgenstein, philosophy is to be regarded not as a body of doctrine but as an activity. The result of philosophizing is not to establish a set of philosophical propositions, but to make other propositions clear.

But even for the Vienna Circle philosophical problems did not disappear so easily. The old perplexities of what is called the theory of knowledge came out again as soon as there was a question of deciding exactly what was meant by a statement's being verifiable. It seemed to follow from the verification principle that a statement of fact could be meaningful to me only if there were a logical — there did not, of course, have to be a practical — possibility of its being tested through my experience. Did it also follow that such statements must in some way refer to my experience? At the outset, the Vienna Circle assumed that it did. In a book called *Der logische Aufbau der Welt* (The Logical Construction of the World), which was published in 1928, Carnap made a heroic, though not, I think, successful attempt to analyse every type of descriptive concept in terms of the single undefined concept of remembered similarity; the effect was to construe all empirical statements as descriptive of the actual or possible course of the subject's experience. The standpoint from which this book was written was called methodological solipsism, the word 'methodological' being put in to show that the solipsism was not to be taken seriously. But here it failed to do its office. The aura of solipsism was not dispersed. For my experience is private to me, and your experience is private to you : how then, if we each have to interpret every statement of fact as referring to our own experience, do we ever succeed in communicating with each other? Schlick's solution of this difficulty was to say that while the content of our experiences is indeed incommunicable, their structure is not. What I call 'red' may look quite different to me from the way what you call 'red' looks to you; we can never tell; it is doubtful even if the question whether they are or are not the same has any meaning. But we can at least discover that we apply the word on the same occasions; so that whatever may be the difference in the content of our private worlds, their structure is the same. This answer has some plausibility, but I do not think that it withstands analysis. It makes things too easy in one respect, and too difficult in another, by starting with the picture of a number of people immured within the several fortresses of their own experience, and then considering what they can convey to one another. Too difficult, because if they really were so immured there would be nothing they could convey, not even structure. Too easy, because if all the statements that I can understand refer to my experience, this must equally be true of the statements which refer to the experiences of others. The walls of my fortress reach out and enclose them.

The difficulties of this problem brought about a serious division of opinion in the Vienna Circle. This dispute, which was conducted mainly in the pages of *Erkenntnis* in the early thirties, became centred on the question of the character and status of what were called 'protocol statements', the basic reports of direct observations, by reference to which the truth of all other empirical statements was supposed to be tested. In opposition to Schlick and Waismann, Neurath and Carnap (who had changed his views on this point under Neurath's influence) maintained that these protocol-statements must, like all other statements of fact, be inter-subjectively verifiable. And this was taken to imply that they must refer to physical events; for it was assumed without argument that physical events were accessible to all alike. So statements which seemed to report the individual's private experience had to be reconstrued as referring to the state of his body, or to his behaviour, in which his use of language was included. The general thesis was that the language of physics, interpreted as containing not merely such sentences as one would expect to find in text-books of physics proper but any sentences which are used to refer to physical events, is a universal language; universal in the sense that every empirical statement can be expressed in it. It was his acceptance of this doctrine of physicalism that led Neurath to insist so much upon the unity of science. It was not only that he wished scientists of different branches to work together more than they do. He believed that, in spite of the differences in their professional vocabularies, they were all fundamentally speaking the same language : they were all investigating the same physical world. This is the old doctrine of materialism, in a modern guise.

The view which had previously been current in the Vienna Circle was that it was through protocol statements that language, as it were, made contact with fact. They alone were verified directly : all other empirical statements were verified indirectly through them. The physicalists, as we have seen, took away from protocol statements their special character as records of experience : and they then went on to deny their function. It makes no sense, they said, to speak of comparing statements with facts. Statements can be compared only with one another. Accordingly, they were led to adopt a coherence theory of truth : they maintained that the criterion by which it is to be decided whether a statement is true is not its correspondence with fact but its consistency with other statements. The classical objection to this type of theory is that many incompatible systems of statements may each be internally consistent : and since they are mutually incompatible they cannot all be true. Carnap's answer to this was that we were to regard as true that system which was accepted by the scientists of our culture circle. But each of the competing systems might consistently contain the *statement* that it alone is accepted by the scientists of our culture circle. What Carnap meant was that the true system was that which they *in fact* accepted. But if a reference to fact is to be allowed in this case, why not in others also ? Experience might even show that contemporary scientists sometimes made mistakes.

I am convinced that the coherence theory of truth is quite untenable. But the thesis of physicalism can be maintained without it. It is quite possible to hold that all empirical statements are to be interpreted physicalistically, without denying that they can correspond with facts. Even so, this thesis is open to serious objections. As applied to one's own experience, it seems to require that one should, as Ramsey put it, feign anaesthesia. It is slightly more plausible as applied to the experiences of others : but however strong the arguments may be which go to show that when we seem to be speaking about the experiences of others we *must* be referring only to their behaviour, the conviction remains that we are not. On any view of philosophy, this inner-outer problem is extremely difficult, and I shall not attempt to give a solution of it here.

In the introduction which he wrote to Wittgenstein's *Tractatus*, Bertrand Russell attributed to Wittgenstein the view that it is impossible to speak about a language in the language itself. I am doubtful if Wittgenstein did hold this — it is one of the points on which he did not make his meaning very clear — but if he did, the Vienna Circle did not follow him. In a book called *Der logische Syntax der Sprache* (The Logical Syntax of Language), of which the original German version appeared in 1934, and an expanded English version in 1936, Carnap showed by working out examples that a language could consistently contain the formulation of its own syntax. It was in this book also that he made his famous distinction between the material and formal modes of speech. A sentence is said to be in the material mode when it expresses a verbal statement which is made to look as if it were factual : translation into the formal mode makes the verbal character of the statement explicit. Thus, to take one of Carnap's examples, if I say 'a rose is a thing', it may be thought that I am making a factual statement like 'roses have thorns'; but what I am really doing is to express, in a misleading way, the syntactical statement that "rose" is a thing-word. Similarly '5 is a number' was said to be more accurately rendered as ' "5" is a numeral', 'he lectured about

Babylon' as 'the word "Babylon" occurred in his lecture'. One reason why Carnap laid great stress upon this point was that he thought that many, if not all, philosophical statements were syntactical, and that they were made unnecessarily difficult by being expressed in the material mode. For instance, the statement 'identity is not a relation between objects' was said by him to be equivalent to 'the symbol of identity is not a descriptive symbol'. 'Time is continuous' to 'The real-number expressions are used as time-co-ordinates'. In general he tended to think that philosophical questions were to be settled by decision; the answers to them depended on the way we chose to construct our language.

A mistake which is sometimes made, even by those who ought to know better, is to assume that Carnap's thesis about the material and formal modes of speech implied that all statements were syntactical, that one could never talk about anything except words. But this was not his view at all. He may have thought that all *philosophical* statements were syntactical, but only a very small proportion of statements are philosophical. Even so he was wrong. What he meant by a syntactical statement was one which was concerned only with the form and order of symbols, as opposed to their meaning, but this does not hold even for his own examples. To say that someone lectured about Babylon is obviously not to say merely, if at all, that he made the noise 'Babylon'. To say that '5' is a numeral, even if it were equivalent to saying that 5 is a number, which it is not, is not to say anything about the shape of the figure '5' but something about its use. To say that 'the symbol of identity is not a descriptive symbol' is again to talk not about the form of the symbol but about the way it is used. In short, these statements are not syntactical but semantic. Carnap himself has come to recognize this and he has brought his logic to bear upon semantics in two of his more recent books. It is not clear to me, however, that the logical study of semantics has yet produced anything of philosophical importance, with the notable exception of Tarski's semantic re-statement of what was rather vaguely implied in the correspondence theory of truth.

It is no doubt true, in some sense, that all philosophical questions are questions about meaning, but merely to say this does not tell us very much. Questions of meaning cover a wide field and there are many different ways of dealing with them. Wittgenstein and Waismann, in their later work, have devoted considerable attention to the ordinary use of words. Carnap, on the other hand, has concentrated rather on building up linguistic systems which may be useful to the scientist. His recent work on probability is fashioned along these lines. Both methods are legitimate and both have produced fruitful results.

It will be seen that the Vienna Circle did not accomplish all that they once hoped. Many of the philosophical problems which they tried to settle still remain unsolved. Perhaps their greatest achievement was to help to introduce a new spirit into philosophy, to set a standard of logical rigour and intellectual responsibility. The producers of what Professor Broad has called 'that grateful and com-

forting mixture of idealistic metaphysics with edify-
ing social and ethical theory' are not extinct. But
in this country at least they are very much on the
defensive: and surely that is something to be
thankful for.

# WITTGENSTEIN

Wittgenstein's second book, *Philosophical Investigations*, presents some of the ideas on which he worked from about 1929 onwards. It was written in German and published in 1953, some two years after his death, with a translation into English by Miss Anscombe. Part I was complete by 1945, and in the Preface Wittgenstein described it as 'the precipitate of philosophical investigations which have occupied me for the last 16 years', *i.e.* since about 1929. The sections of it are numbered, and I give in order at the foot of each page the numbers of those from which I quote.

HE follows Moore in the defence of common sense and in a regard for our ordinary language; but criticizes the notion of *analysis* in a way that has quite changed philosophy. He writes of every sentence in our language as being '"in order as it is"', claims that 'philosophy may in no way interfere with the actual use of language', and declares that 'what *we* do' in philosophy 'is to bring words *back* from their metaphysical to their everyday usage'. That is, 'when philosophers use a word — "knowledge", "being", "object", "I", "proposition", "name" — and try to grasp the *essence* of the thing, we must always ask : is the word ever *actually* used in this way in the language which is its original home'. In such cases 'we must stick to the subjects

[1] Cf. Moore, *Defence of Common Sense*, 198 : 'I am maintaining that all the propositions . . . are *wholly* true'.

---

98, 124, 116.

of our everyday thinking, and not go astray and imagine that we have to describe extreme subtleties';[1] we must 'look into the workings of our language'. The confusions which occupy us arise not when our language is 'doing work' but when it is 'like an engine idling'.

With Moore, Wittgenstein shared also a sympathy for metaphysical philosophers. Where there exists a prejudice which stands in the way of seeing how a word is actually used, it is often 'not a *stupid* prejudice', for 'the problems arising through a misinterpretation of our forms of language have the character of *depth* : they are deep disquietudes ; their roots are as deep in us as the forms of our language, and their importance is as great as the importance of our language'. These philosophers have, when at their best, 'run their heads up against the limits of language'.

And Wittgenstein emphasized, with Moore, 'our strange position', that we know what many words and phrases mean even though 'no philosopher hitherto', or anyone else, has succeeded in setting out in detail what they mean ; we are constantly failing to see *our* use of this and that word clearly ; but in our philosophical investigations we are trying to understand the functions and structures of *our* language ; we are trying to look into the workings of *our* language in such a way as to make us recognize those workings. Compare Moore's formulation :

[1] Cf. Moore, 'I am not using the expressions in any such *subtle* sense. I meant by them precisely what any reader in reading them will have understood me to mean.'

106, 109, 132, 340, 111, 119, 100, 92, 109.

'my main object here has been to try to *make* the reader see it'.

Here, at this point, Wittgenstein parts wholly from Moore. We must 'make a radical break with the idea that language always functions in *one* way, always serves the *same* purpose : to convey thoughts — which may be about houses, pains, good and evil, or anything else you please'. It is just such a picture that '*stands in the way of our seeing* the use of the word as it is'.

Moore had, in 1903, written of certain difficulties in philosophy as if they were like difficulties in vision, in seeing something clearly; of a philosophical investigation as like a visual investigation, a visual scrutiny. Moore had thought: it is like trying to discern something of a kind difficult to see, such as air or clear water in a stream. (I may see it all of a sudden by a fleeting ripple.) Or it is like coming to see by a careful scrutiny that what in an X-ray plate I took for one shadow is two. Moore wrote, for example, 'the other element "consciousness" is extremely difficult to fix . . . seems to escape us . . . seems transparent; we look through it'; [1] and (to take an example of the other kind of difficulty) the Idealist 'fails to see that esse and percipi are *distinct*, are *two* at all'.

Naturally enough Moore's remedy for a philosophical difficulty *so* described was this : to look still more attentively at what is *before his mind* just *at the time when* he asks the question. 'If we look *attentively*

[1] Moore, *Refutation of Idealism*, 20.

304, 305

enough, it can be distinguished'; 'whoever will
*attentively* consider with himself *what is before his mind*'
can 'come to recognize' that he has there not one
object but two. Of such an account Wittgenstein
wrote : we imagine 'that we have to describe extreme
subtleties'.

Yet Moore admits that 'the moment we try to
fix our attention on consciousness, to see what *dis-
tinctly* it is, it seems to vanish'. On which Wittgenstein notes that 'it is as if one had altered the adjust-
ment of a microscope'; or 'we feel as if we had to
repair a torn spider's web with our fingers'.

Moore's kind of picture of a philosophical
problem is characterized by Wittgenstein as follows :
It is as if in our usual forms of expression there were
'something *hidden* that has to be brought to light',
and we often go so far as to 'think we already see it
there'. The picture is of 'something that lies
*within*, which we *see* when we look into the thing;
something that lies *beneath the surface*, and which an
analysis *digs out*'.

But, says Wittgenstein, the attempt at 'scrutiny'
results not in a digging up of something from beneath,
but in our coming only on things which we think of
as mere surface phenomena, and not refined enough
to be what we are looking for. Take as an example
scrutiny of an intention : 'For a moment I intended
to . . .' That is, I had a particular feeling, an inner
experience; and I remember it. But I am urged,
'And now remember quite precisely!' At this the
'*inner* experience of intending seems to vanish again.
*Instead* one remembers thoughts, feelings, movements,

---

106, 25, 645, 106, 91, 101, 92, 645, 436.

and also connexions with earlier situations'; what, in this context, one had the inclination to treat as mere superficial accompaniments.

Wittgenstein describes this part of Moore's position as 'that *dead-end* in philosophy, where one believes that the difficulty of the task consists in this: our having to describe phenomena that are *hard to get hold of*, the present experience that slips quickly by, or something of that kind. Where we find ordinary language too crude, and it looks as if we were having to do not with phenomena of every-day but with ones that "*easily elude us*".'

But the fact is that 'the picture of the inner process', so far from 'giving us the correct idea of the *use*' of the word 'intend', '*stands in the way* of our seeing the use of the word as it is'. Concentrated on looking for the hidden which we think is there, we have no attention to spare for what lies openly around us.

We are bewitched too by an inadequate conception of what it is for something 'to be hidden'. What we are looking for is indeed 'hidden'; but not by being behind something else, or difficult to dig out, or difficult to discriminate sharply from something else, or transparent. What is hidden in that way is of no interest to us. We have over-looked a no less common way in which a thing, or movement, may be concealed from us. 'The decisive movement in the conjuring trick has been made, and it was *the very one that we thought quite innocent*.'

The things we are looking for 'already lie open

305, 126, 416, 92, 93, 94, 97.

to view', and have 'escaped remark only because they are always before our eyes'. Expecting something queer, we go in pursuit of chimeras; looking for something with a halo, we miss the humble; dazzled by the thought of the ideal, we fail to see clearly the actual. 'Philosophy is a battle against the *bewitchment* of our intelligence', not, as Moore and other analysts thought, against defective vision or wandering attention. It is a poor conjurer who has to have the lights turned low.

Just as, in Moore's view, Idealists had failed to realize how complex is the concept of *spirit*, so Moore, in Wittgenstein's view, has failed to realize how complex is such a concept as *consciousness*.[1] Moore and others have purified it, refined it, 'sublimed' it, looking at it only when it is 'idling'; have failed to 'be struck by' what no doubt they already clearly see, the complex and varied use of the phrase 'conscious of', taking these, the true circumstances of its use, to be merely 'its coarser accompaniments'. 'The criteria which we accept for "being able to", "understanding" are much more complicated than might appear at first sight. The role of these words in our language is other, *more involved, than we are tempted to think*.' But 'this *role* is what we have to understand in order to resolve philosophical paradoxes. And hence *definitions* usually fail to resolve them; so, a fortiori does the assertion that a word is "*indefinable*".'

Moore is again a target of Wittgenstein's account

---

[1] *Refutation of Idealism*, 20.

100, 109, 153, 182.

of the philosopher who, pointing to an object in front of him, says 'This is here', and claims that the sentence makes sense to him : 'he should ask himself in what *special* circumstances this sentence is *actually* used', for there it does make sense.

Analytic philosophers, in short, no less than metaphysical ones, must be made to bring words back from philosophical to actual everyday usage, to their use in the language which is their original home.

Everything we need for our problems lies open to view, and philosophy simply puts everything before us. It aims to give the wide presentation we need of the facts of usage, and 'may in no way interfere with the actual usage of language ; it can in the end only describe it. It leaves everything as it is.' A man (perhaps myself) may be 'unable to look and see how, for example, *propositions* work', or the word 'conscious', or 'this'. Very well, then, we must make him (make myself) look and see it. 'We must do away with all explanation, and *description alone* must take its place.'

Yet philosophy is not just any description of uses of language, however extensive, various, and exact. Such a description only 'gets its purpose *from the philosophical problems*'. It is not enough to turn our attention away from the sublimed, indiscernible essence and accommodate our sight to the multitudinous ordinary ; or to loosen our too concentrated gaze from what is at this moment immediately in front of our mind, and spread our attention so that we see also circumstances before and after. In the crowd of circumstances thus seen, I may still remain

117, 116, 126, 122, 124, 93, 109.

every bit as lost as before. 'A philosophical problem has the form : "I don't know my way about".' I may be lost even when I see clearly everything that is around me.

As we learn our language and employ it we do not thereby acquire any wide, extensive view of the uses which make it up, and how they stand to one another. But for every problem it is of basic importance to *acquire* such a wide-ranging familiarity with some regions of usage; to assemble many facts of usage, and command a wide view. 'The work of the philosopher consists in *assembling reminders* for a particular purpose'; but not only in that, for though I should assemble a multitude I might become even more lost than before, I might even less 'know my way about'.

Besides *assembling* reminders, sketches, I must *select* and *arrange* them, in such a way that I come to get some *picture* of the landscape. The very nature of philosophical investigation compels a man to travel over a wide region of uses, criss-cross in every direction, the same use being approached again and again, each time from a different direction, from a different point of view, from a different use. These various sketches do not of themselves fall together to form a picture, or even a map, of a place or region; they have to *be* arranged 'so that if you looked at them you could *get* a picture' of the landscape there, and so to some extent get to 'know your way about'.

'Hence the importance of *finding* and *inventing* intermediate cases.' Only by this *finding, inventing,*

123, 127. Preface, ix; 122.

95

and *arranging* of views, not by an inactive observation of all equally that happens to come before my eye, do I get to know my way about and 'out of the fly-bottle'. The 'essence', so to speak, becomes 'surveyable', not by 'digging out', 'analysis', and not by passive watching of what 'already lies open to view', but 'by a rearrangement', or several, which I have to make.

Instead of concentrating into a gaze, I am to make a wide survey; and it is not that cases just come before me in their arrangement, for there are cases to be invented by me and arrangements of them to be made by me. Here is why Wittgenstein presents no method in philosophy; there is no method for inventing cases, no method for arranging them.

And there is no method for '*being struck by*' one fact rather than another. Yet no matter how much detail about a use we may methodically assemble, we may, and commonly do, 'fail to be struck by what, once seen, is *most* striking and most powerful'. The fly in the fly-bottle may countless times eye the way out — and not be particularly struck by it.

Wittgenstein did not think that all philosophical problems must arise only from ordinary language. He says merely that the most widespread ones do. But he knew well that the specialized language of any subject is liable to give rise to philosophical problems. In such a case, to bring a word back to its actual use, is to bring it back to its actual use in that specialized language, however unordinary, that is its original home. He himself worked on philosophical problems which arise in mathematics, not much of which enters into ordinary language.

92, 129.

# CONSTRUCTION AND ANALYSIS

IN earlier lectures in this series, Mr. Pears has described the metaphysics of Logical Atomism; Professor Ayer has set out the programme of Logical Positivism; and Mr. Paul has spoken of the work of Professor Moore in Cambridge from 1900. You will perhaps have noticed that, in spite of their differences, Atomists, Positivists, and Professor Moore all have something in common, even if it is only a word, to be pronounced with approval. The word is 'analysis'. Certainly they did not all have exactly the same conception of analysis. Wittgenstein, in the *Tractatus*, gave no indication of thinking that analysis into the ultimate elements could actually be carried out; nor did he indicate at all clearly what he thought the ultimate elements were. The Positivists, on the other hand, were less non-committal. They had the ultimate elements clearly identified as 'sense-contents'; and they thought that at least the principles of analysis could be laid down, even if the details could not always be filled in. Atomists and Positivists alike accepted the skeleton language of the new mathematical logic as providing the formal structure of the ultimate and penultimate statements. Professor Moore stands rather apart from the members of both these groups. For he was not committed, as they were, to ultimate elements, nor was he tied so closely to the forms of mathematical logic; he was not bound, as they were, by a foreknowledge of the pattern to be revealed. For him, analysis was not the instrument of a wholesale metaphysics, but the method of a piecemeal elucidation. For him, analysis was not a programme, but a practice.

But what exactly did those who prescribed or practised philosophical analysis, *mean* by this expression? In particular, what were they claiming to analyse? Was it, for example, *sentences*, of the indicative or assertive kind? Or was it the meanings of those sentences — by some, rather unhappily, called *propositions*? Or was it the *thoughts* or *beliefs* which the sentences expressed? Or the *statements* they were used to make? It does not matter much, now, which we say; though each of these answers may, in its own way, be misleading. Analysis of sentences, for example, suggests the grammarian; analysis of thoughts or beliefs, the psychologist; and analysis of statements, perhaps the policeman or the advocate. Maybe it is best to say, as Moore always said, that the objects of analysis were propositions. This answer, whatever its shortcomings, emphasizes, without over-emphasizing, the linguistic nature of the enterprise, the preoccupation with meaning. For, however we describe the objects of analysis, particular analyses, whether given in detail or sketched in outline, always looked much the same. A sentence, representative of a class of sentences belonging to the same topic, was supposed to be elucidated by the framing of another sentence. This second sentence was to be more or less equivalent in meaning to the first, but was to make explicit at least some of the complexities of meaning concealed by the verbal form of the first. Presumably, for those who held that analysis had a terminus in logical atoms, there would exist, in theory, for every sentence of common speech, a *final* analysis — a sentence in which *all* complexities of meaning would be made *completely* explicit, in terms of the ultimate logical elements. Not that all analyses were thought of as reducing the complex to simpler elements. Some were thought of, rather, as a *recasting* of the verbal form of a sentence in such a way as to reveal the logical affinities of the proposition it expressed, and to dispel the illusion of other logical affinities which it did not really possess. It was as if propositions belonged to logical families, most of the members of each of which wore a certain kind of verbal dress; but some members of some families masqueraded in the verbal clothing characteristic of other families; and had to be re-garbed to prevent confusion. This, too, was the task of analysis.

So, then, the general conception of analysis was that of a kind of translation, or, perhaps better, a kind of paraphrase. For it was to be translation within a language, not from one language to another : a translation from a less explicit to a more explicit form, or from a misleading to an unmisleading form. If your problem was, say, the nature of *truth*, or, say, the nature of *existence*, you hoped to solve it by finding a formula for translating sentences in which the adjective 'true' or the verb 'exists' occurred, into sentences in which these expressions did not occur, and in which no straightforward synonyms of them occurred either. Nor was this, after all, so very revolutionary a conception of philosophy. The search for definitions of problematic ideas was almost as old as philosophy itself. What was new was rather the substitution of sentences for words, of propositions for concepts, as the unit upon which analysis was to be practised. And for this change, as earlier lectures have shown, there were very good reasons.

Although, in Cambridge, Wittgenstein was already doing something very different, on the whole the method of analysis dominated English philosophy in the thirties. It brought some advances in some fields. But in the main the results were disappointing. The sentences of common speech seemed somehow to resist the simplifying expansions which theory had prepared for them. Even Russell's earlier brilliant glosses on the structure of ordinary sentences, in terms of the syntax of the new formal logic, began in the end to seem a little queer. And those who went to work with fewer preconceptions about their results were apt to find that if they preserved the sense of the original, they achieved no simplification : and that if they gained a simplification, they did so at the cost of losing the sense.

So what was to be done ? Philosophers sought understanding of the concepts which were the apparatus of our thinking. They looked — and this seemed natural enough — to the propositions, the sentences, in which these concepts found their employment, the sentences in which we commonly express our thoughts and beliefs. But if these sentences resisted translation into more perspicuous forms, what was to be done? Well, of course, there were many possibilities. But, among them, two have been of dominant importance in post-war philosophizing. One involves turning away from the forms of common speech, while preserving much of the apparatus of the original programme of analysis. The other involves continued close attention to the forms of common speech, together with a vastly altered and extended conception of the nature and techniques of analysis.

Let me say more about these two contrasting courses. The first method, incidentally, is pursued mainly in America, and is associated especially with the names of Carnap and Quine. The second method is pursued mainly in England, and is associated especially with the names of Austin and Ryle. For the sake of convenience, I may speak of the American School and the English School. But I need hardly say that the titles cover quite wide divergences between individuals. The main inspiration of the American School is still, as it was for the Logical Atomists, the new formal logic, due to Frege and Russell. For this logic provides a skeleton language in which the meaning of every element is absolutely precise, and the articulation of the elements absolutely clear. By using this framework, this basic linguistic apparatus, other systems of concepts can be constructed in which the mutual relationships of the parts will have just the same clarity and precision as in formal logic itself. Of course, systems so constructed, and indeed the logical system itself used in their construction, are not natural growths, like the language of daily life, but artificial creations. But just in this very fact, it is claimed, lies the philosophical superiority of system-construction over the attempt to analyse ordinary language. That attempt, it is suggested, is defeated by the looseness, the untidiness, the shifting complexities of common speech. Instead of pursuing it, then, we are to construct clear models of language in which all the essential logical relations of our concepts can be made plain, while the irrevelant tangles of actual usage are cut away. Of course, some preliminary or incidental remark will have to be made, connecting key expressions of the system with expressions we ordinarily use. Otherwise it would not be clear what the system was about, what concepts it was intended to clarify. But once these points of contact are made, the system stands on its own, a precise and rigid structure to which our ordinary conceptual equipment is a rough and confusing approximation. The system of formal logic is itself the greatest of all achievements of this kind, as well as being the prerequisite of others. For it reveals the underlying structure of all our thinking. From those little logical words which are indispensable to all developed discourse — words such as 'the', 'a', 'all', 'some', 'if', 'not ', 'or', 'and', 'is' — it distils what is essential and discards the troublesome remainder. Formal logic is the model for other philosophical models, as well as the framework on which the others are to be built.

Very roughly, that is the case, or an important part of the case, for system-construction as a method in philosophy. Evidently, it has its appeal. It offers something clear and orderly, in the place of something apparently confused and imprecise. It is not only attractive, but plausible. For there are many things which can be better understood as a result of the construction of a simplified model of their working; and why should not the concepts which exercise philosophers be among these things?

But the case for the alternative method can also be made to sound very plausible. After all, we are seeking to gain an understanding of the concepts and categories in terms of which we carry on our thinking; not only, or primarily, our advanced and technical thinking, but our common, daily thinking. For it is the most general, most fundamental and most ordinary ideas which give rise to the major problems of philosophy. Is it, after all, so reasonable to think that our ordinary use of language blurs and distorts these ordinary ideas? For common speech is subjected to the severest of all tests for efficiency, as a medium for the expression and communication of our thoughts — the test of constant use. If we want to understand the habits and way of life of an animal, we must carefully observe his behaviour in his natural surroundings; it is no good turning our backs on his actual behaviour, constructing a clock-work model from an engineer's designs and then studying that. So with our concepts. If we want to know how they work, we must watch them at work. As for the failure of the original programme of analysis, as applied to the sentences of common speech, the fault there lay not in common speech, but in a too rigid and too narrow conception of analysis. Why should it be supposed that the only way to gain understanding of the words which express the philosophically puzzling concepts was to translate sentences in which they occurred into sentences in which they did not occur? The belief in the exclusive efficacy of this method is just the troublesome legacy of discredited theories. It is too rigid a conception of analysis, because it supposes the existence of exact quasi-definitional relations between classes of concepts, which do not in fact obtain. It is too narrow, because it neglects altogether very many quite different features of the functioning of language, which it is of the first importance accurately to note and describe, if our philosophical problems are to be resolved. And the programme of system-construction suffers from just these same limitations. For it, too, confines itself to exhibiting quasi-definitional relations between constructed concepts. Admittedly the relations do really obtain in the constructed system; because they are made to. But even this limited success is purchased at too high a price : the price of divorce from the conceptual realities of common speech. So, for the old, limited and theory-ridden programme of analysis, we are to substitute a different aim : that of coming to understand philosophically puzzling concepts by carefully and accurately noting the ways in which the related linguistic expressions are actually used in discourse. Of course, not all features of the use of these expressions will be relevant to the philosopher's task. It is his special skill to discern *which* are relevant, and *how* they are relevant.

I have presented these two views of philosophical method as if they were in sharp and irreconcilable conflict. And, indeed, the partisans of each frequently enough write and speak as if this were so. But it is in fact not so clear that the philosophical builders of artificial languages, and the philosophical investigators of natural language, must necessarily be each other's enemies. Up to a point, at least, each method may be seen as the complementary of the other. For, on the one hand, the simplicities of a constructed model may cast light, if only by contrast, on the complexities of actual usage; and, on the other hand, some observation of the workings of natural language seems necessary for the successful construction of the simplified model. So it might seem that the situation calls for co-operation rather than competition. And so, up to a point, it does. Yet I am partisan enough to want to upset a little the symmetry of this friendly picture — or perhaps I should say, cautious enough to want to delimit spheres of influence. And, to explain my reasons for this, I shall have to try to fill a notable gap in what I have so far said. I shall have, that is, to say something about the general nature of philosophical problems, and of philosophical understanding. I shall have to say what I think the philosopher's tasks are.

There is one task about which there will be little disagreement. Sometimes, instead of just setting our concepts and speech-forms to work in the ordinary way, we reflect upon them, or with them, at a level of unusual generality; and when we do so, we may find ourselves driven towards conclusions not simply bizarre, not simply shocking to common sense, but somehow intrinsically unacceptable; and intrinsically unacceptable because at variance with the ordinary use, and hence with the ordinary meaning, of the very words in which we are tempted to express them. Yet such conclusions may seem, though un-acceptable, inescapable. In this situation, some conceptual distortion has taken place; and, in general, the distortion is the consequence of an undue pressure exercised by *some* only of the features of the language in which we express the concept in question, to the temporary exclusion of others. To correct the distortion, we must clearly expose the full logical workings of the distorted concept, and perhaps of others too; and locate, if we can, the source of the distorting pressure. This is one of the tasks confronting the critical philosopher; and is worthy of a first mention, because so much of philosophy begins with paradox and the resolution of paradox. But it would itself be a paradox to represent the whole task of philosophy as the correction of philosophical mistakes. Even if such mistakes provide the initial impulse to this conceptual anatomy, the enterprise then acquires its own momentum and may be pursued for its own sake. There may be pure research as well as *ad hoc* therapy. So the philosopher may undertake a more detailed examination, a more systematic ordering and description, of speech-forms, of types of discourse, of types of concept, than would be necessary simply to relieve the pressures of paradox.

This is still not all that may be required of the philosopher. So far I have represented him as trying to exhibit the ways in which our concepts and forms of thought actually operate — partly for the sake of doing so, partly for the sake of clearing up conceptual confusions, diagnosing philosophical disorders. But there are other and more imaginative sides to his activity, not strictly separable from these, but distinguishable from them. For fully to understand our conceptual equipment, it is not enough to know, to be able to say, how it works. We want to know also *why* it works as it does. To ask this is to ask to be shown how the nature of our thinking is rooted in the nature of the world and in our own natures. This is not an impossible enquiry; for it is quite possible to imagine our experience being different in fundamental ways, and then to consider how our conceptual apparatus might naturally be adjusted to accommodate these differences. In seeing this, we see also how our concepts, as they are, are rooted in the world, as it is. This kind of thinking might be called the explanatory work of the philosophical imagination. There is another kind of thinking which might be called the creative or constructive work of the philosophical imagination. To engage in this kind of thinking is to consider how, without the nature of the world being fundamentally different, we might nevertheless view it through the medium of a different conceptual apparatus, might conduct our discourse about it in forms different from, though related to, those which we actually use. Evidently, both these kinds of imaginative philosophical thinking are complementary to the analytical kinds I first distinguished. In practice, each kind tends to be so interwoven with the others that there is a certain artificiality in so distinguishing them. But it is not wholly artificial. For one strand or another may be decisively dominant in any one piece of work, or in the work of any one philosopher. Let me, for convenience, give names to these different strands in philosophical thought. In the order in which I first mentioned them, I shall distinguish the analytical strands into the therapeutic and the systematic; and the imaginative strands into the explanatory and the inventive.

And now, I think, we are in a better position to assess the relative claims of the English and American schools in post-war philosophy. For the task of therapeutic analysis, as I have described it, it is obvious that the methods of the English school are of primary importance — while the method of system-construction is, at best, of secondary helpfulness. For the paradoxes and perplexities in question had their root in a vivid, but imperfect, picture of the working of the concepts concerned — in a kind of caricature of their logical features. The only fully rational method of correction here is to replace the caricature with an accurate delineation of those features, which will show how the caricature distorted, what it exaggerated and what it missed out. And it is in the actual use of the linguistic expressions for the concepts concerned, and nowhere else, that we find the data from which we can draw this accurate picture. A simplified diagram from which the puzzle-generating features are, perhaps, absent, is here no substitute, though it may be a help. What of systematic analysis? This, as I described it, was simply a more generalized and systematic attempt to distinguish and describe the logical features of our concepts and speech-forms. Its data, therefore, and its methods are fundamentally the same as those of therapeutic analysis, though it has not the same anxious concern with possible sources of perplexity and paradox. There may appear to be

a slight oddity in speaking of systematic analysis of
language and then declaring that the way to pursue
it is not by the constructing of linguistic systems.
But if this does seem odd, it is only a superficial
oddity. For evidently there is a difference between
constructing a segment of artificial language and
systematically describing the workings of a slice of
natural language. One must not exaggerate the
difference. The task of tracing patterns in living
language is difficult, and would be almost impossible
if one were not allowed to do a little regimenting.
Still the difference remains a vital one. The living
creatures of language, even when mildly regimented,
are still seen as performing a range of functions of
immense diversity; whereas only a few of these
functions can be imitated by the logical machines
built by the constructionist.

What of the imaginative side of philosophy?
Obviously neither a facility in the techniques of
system-construction, nor a keen eye for the linguistic
facts is of direct help in the *explanatory* task. But
when we turn to the *inventive* or *constructive* side —
one might almost say, the metaphysical side — the
case is different. The system-builder, guided by
certain ideals of quasi-mathematical elegance and
exactness, provides us with models of ways in which
we might have thought and talked, had we been less
complex and many-levelled creatures than we are.
In doing so, he may, as I have already said, cast
much direct and indirect light on fundamental
features of the ways in which we actually do think
and talk. And this is not all. A philosopher's
systematic reconstruction of concepts and speech-

forms may sometimes have an application in other branches of knowledge than philosophy. It may provide useful, and even indispensable, tools for the advance of mathematics and the more mathematical sciences. And here again there is a parallel with the inventive speculations of more traditional metaphysics. What begins as metaphysics may end as science. But this is not its only justification; and it is time to drop the prim pragmatism which pretends that it is.

So, then, the appearance of a deathly struggle between these two methods in contemporary philosophy is, in part at least, a misleading appearance, an illusion. The illusion is not necessarily regrettable : it may act as a spur to effort on both sides. And it is not wholly illusion; for there is here something of a clash, almost of temperament — between the desire to understand what exists, and the desire to make something new and, in some sense, better. Nevertheless, the apparent conflict is largely an illusion, even if a useful one. For the two methods are not rival ways of attaining just the same end — ways of which one must be quite wrong if the other is quite right. They are, partly, complementary methods of achieving one end; and, partly, both of them, appropriate and closely related methods of achieving different, though closely related, ends. For me to say which of these different ends I considered the more important would have no more interest than any other expression of personal preference; but it may not be altogether fanciful to find in the *national* preferences which I mentioned earlier, some indication of a characteristic difference between the New World and the Old.

# ANALYSIS AND IMAGINATION

In this final lecture I want to amplify and extend some of the remarks which Mr. Strawson made towards the end of his contribution to this series. By doing this I hope to make a little clearer where philosophy now is, and where — perhaps — it might go next. But prophecy is notoriously a dangerous trade, and in this case not a particularly useful one; so that my aim will be rather to indicate where paths are to be found than to venture a prediction about which of them will actually be followed. And I ought to make at once the unreluctant admission that I make no claim at all to be a spokesman for all or even most philosophers, even in this country, or even in Oxford. My way of looking at the present situation is, I am sure, not very eccentric, and not, I hope, unduly partisan; I believe, of course, that it is the right view to take; but no reading whatever would be likely to satisfy all parties. I do not think that this is really a matter for regret or apology; in any case it cannot be helped, but must simply be admitted and remembered.

You will remember that Mr. Strawson, towards the end of his lecture, offered a brief account of what he took to be the philosopher's tasks, and for these tasks he devised a rough system of classification. He first distinguished between the critical, or analytic, and the imaginative tasks of philosophy, and then further divided each of these into two — the analytic aspect into the therapeutic and the systematic, the imaginative aspect into the explanatory and the inventive. I propose to take these four subdivisions in order, attempting to characterize in reasonable detail the types of philosophical activity in question. This suspiciously tidy method of proceeding should not be taken too seriously, but will, I hope, prove useful enough to justify its slight artificiality.

First, then, therapeutic analysis. This name itself, with its clinical metaphor, vividly expresses a now widely held view of the nature of some philosophical problems. This view is by no means completely new. Berkeley, for instance, in the early eighteenth century, seems often to have had the idea that philosophers' problems are like afflictions to be cured, or like mental knots to be untied, rather than like straight questions to be given straight answers. But this idea of Berkeley's did not take root at the time, and its wide diffusion today is due pre-eminently to the later work of Wittgenstein. Wittgenstein himself sometimes spoke of the puzzled philosopher as a victim of 'cramp'; and how often one hears philosophers today speak of the 'diagnosis' of philosophical difficulties, as if they were a kind of intellectual disease. The idea behind the metaphors is this. Sometimes, instead of simply using our concepts, our language, in thinking and talking about ordinary affairs, we are inclined to raise questions of unusually high generality, sometimes questions actually *about* the concepts that we normally use in thinking about other things. We ask, for instance, not, as historians might, 'How can we know what Gladstone really thought about Socialism?' but 'How can we know what anybody really thinks about anything? How can we know that they think at all?': or again, 'How can we ever know *anything* about the past?' or even 'What *is* knowledge? What *is* the past?' And here one enormous danger is that of mistaken assimilations. We are liable to have, probably without realizing that we have them, preconceived ideas about how words and concepts must function, taking perhaps some particular examples as typical or standard; and then we are tempted to assume that *all* cases must clearly or covertly resemble this preconceived type, we try to describe them as if this were so. For example, we may take as a standard case of knowledge my knowing that there is a cat on the mat now before me. And from this we may find ourselves led on to say that, if we are to have knowledge of the past, it must in some way be present before us (but how could that be?); or that all we can really know about another person is what his body does and what noises come out of his mouth (but can that be all?) Again, with the general idea that active verbs describe actions, we may come to ask 'What action am I performing, when I know?'; or with the idea that adjectives stand for properties, we may come to ask 'What property is it that we ascribe to an event, when we say that it is past? And how can we possibly become acquainted with this property?'

The difficulties that result from these questions are not due to any kind of ignorance, to an ordinary

THE REVOLUTION IN PHILOSOPHY

lack of sufficient information to answer them. They
are due to the distorted character of the questions
themselves. It is rather as if one asked, not 'What
is a screw-driver?' but 'What sort of chisel is a
screw-driver?' — embodying in the question itself
the requirement that something must be described
as what it is not, assimilated to something which in
fact it does not resemble. Wittgenstein observes
that we are apt to fall into these traps when our
language is 'idling' or 'on holiday'; the idea that
knowing is some sort of action does not occur to us
in *using* the word 'know', but is apt to assail us when
we try to *describe* its use; the feeling that the past is
either the present or nothing does not beset the
working historian, but crops up when we think about
the past in wholly general terms. This amounts to
the hard but true saying that questions having the
characteristic generality of philosophical questions
are peculiarly apt to draw from us nonsensical
answers. The remedy is to put our concepts back to
work again in actual examples, to observe how in
concrete cases they do actually function. The
danger, the cause of philosophical 'cramp', is the
belief that there *must* be resemblances where in fact
there are not; it is by unmasking this belief, by confronting it with the actual complexity of the facts,
that our cramps may be eased, our disorders
diagnosed. If it seems to us that knowledge of the
past is mysterious or impossible, we need to be
reminded of what in fact it is to have knowledge of
the past, how it differs from knowing about the
present, and how though we cannot know everything we do know a good deal. We need to have

our attention recalled to the concrete and the familiar.

I think that there can now be no doubt at all that this view of the genesis of some philosophical problems, and the consequent view about how to deal with them, have made a permanent and immensely important contribution not only to the current practice of philosophy, but also to the proper understanding of its history.

Let us pass on now to what Mr. Strawson called the 'systematic' work of analytic philosophy. So far the scrutiny of the concepts we employ, examination of the complexities of language, has been envisaged as being undertaken for a particular purpose — the purpose, namely, of breaking down the cramping rigidities which generate some philosophical difficulties. But, as Mr. Strawson observed, our examination need not always be undertaken for this particular purpose; we do not *have* to begin with an existing philosophical knot, and stop as soon as it seems to have come untied; we may examine language in the spirit of pure research, describing and ordering its features with no other essential aim than to do just this.

Now this programme is not, it appears, uncontroversial. There are some who say that it is trivial and boring; there are some who say that it is impossible; and there are others who say simply that it is not philosophy. I do not myself find any of these charges impressive. If one is assured that the systematic study of language is boring, what can one do but confess that one does not find it so? If one is told that it serves no practical purpose, what can one do but say 'No, of course not'? The second objection, that systematic study of language is really not possible, is more interesting. The suggestion is that language is both so fluid and so complex that it is recalcitrant to any classification; it presents a fatal dilemma between artificial regimentation and an endless piling up of constantly shifting distinctions. However, this view seems unreasonably pessimistic. Comparatively little such study of language has in fact been attempted, and it is hard to see good reason for adopting a defeatist posture in advance. On the contrary, I would not mind at this point venturing the prediction that this little-trodden path will be trodden to some purpose before very long.

This leaves us with the fairly common contention that systematic research into the functioning of language is not philosophy. This contention is interesting in one way, and intolerably boring in another way. It is interesting because it may throw into prominence the conception of philosophy which the objector has; but it is boring because nothing really turns on it except the application of a name. Few people would wish to deny that therapeutic analysis deserves the name of philosophy, nor could it be denied that the systematic extension of this interest in language is both natural and desirable; and so, if there is such work to be done, need one wrangle about what the doing of it is to be called?

In any case I would like to pass on now to what we have called the imaginative tasks of philosophy, which we further distinguished as the explanatory and the inventive. These raise rather more intricate questions, but both clearly crop up quite naturally out of the enquiries I have just been describing. Just as a limited interest in language, pursued for the purpose of resolving philosophical paradox, leads quite naturally to a general study of language for its own sake, so the study of how our language functions leads quite naturally to the two questions: *Why* do we use our language in this way? and, What would it be like if we used it differently (or, used a different kind of language)? To take the explanatory aspect first. I will try to give an example of the sort of problem I have in mind. There is a number of long-standing and notorious puzzles which turn on the concept of *causation*. In the course of attempting to draw the sting from these puzzles, we are inevitably led to enquire what exactly our concept of causation is; how, and in how many ways, do we employ the word 'cause' itself and the rest of our very extensive causal vocabulary? Suppose now that we know the answers to these questions; suppose that we have charted to our satisfaction the most important features of the concept of causation. Now it may well occur to us that there are some features of this concept which need explaining — *why* should it have the features which we discern in it? For example: Hume in a justly celebrated passage observes that, if two events are causally connected, there must be a 'constant conjunction' between them; but, as he saw, this is not enough to distinguish the cause from the effect; we must add that the cause must be the earlier in time of the two. Now why should this be? If the events are indeed constantly conjoined, the relation between them is so far symmetrical — why should we distinguish the earlier as the cause, and refuse to entertain the idea that the later might just as well be called the cause of the first? Here it seems natural to say that we rely upon causal connections in our attempts to make things happen and prevent things from happening; we are interested in what can be done *now* to influence the future, whereas nothing that happens now could influence the past. It is sense to say that an event made a later event happen, but it would make no sense to say that an event made an *earlier* event *have* happened. But already two important steps have been taken here: first, we have brought in the empirical point that *in fact* we are concerned to influence the course of events, and second, we have run into the conceptual point that, while it makes sense to speak of influencing the future, it does not make sense to speak of influencing the past. And here in turn we might raise the question why our conceptual apparatus should have *this* feature. But we need not elaborate the example. It is, I imagine, clear enough already what sort of questions are liable to come up. To explain our concept of causation we need to trace its connections not only with other concepts that we employ, but also with empirical facts about the course of events in the world and the ways in which we concern ourselves with those events.

Now about this sort of explanation there remains a great deal to be thought out. Two things at least seem to me beyond question. One is that such explanations are immensely worth having. One's sense of having achieved a firm, rational grasp of some feature of our thought or language is enormously increased if one can say, not only that it has this feature, but also why it should have it. Indeed, if one cannot say the latter, one is hardly entitled to claim understanding. The second thing that seems to me certain is that there must be such explanations to be found. For after all, except in certain exceptional areas, there is nothing artificial about language, and it is most unlikely that it should have taken on the shapes that it has if there were not very good reasons why it should have taken on those shapes. However, I think it is at present less clear what exactly is involved in offering explanations of this kind, or by what sort of tests we are to decide on their merits. It is not usually a matter of discovering new and recondite facts, but rather a matter of noticing, and seeing the relevance of, familiar facts. But how is one to see which facts are relevant? Mr. Strawson mentioned briefly one natural device. One may imagine the world, or our circumstances in the world, to be changed in some way or other, and ask one's self how this imagined change might require some modification of our conceptual apparatus. Suppose, for instance, that our senses of sight and touch were very much less acute than they are, while our senses of hearing and smell were immensely sharpened; or suppose that we commonly lived our lives in total darkness, or by various types of artificial light — how might such changes be expected to modify our concepts of colour, of sound, of space, or of material things? If we can see how imagined changes of circumstances might modify our concepts, we may come to see how our concepts as they actually are depend on the circumstances which actually obtain.

The important difficulties in this are three. First, it is sometimes hard to describe fully and coherently the change of circumstances that one wishes to consider — the very fact that the change might be expected to modify our language puts an obstacle in the way of describing it in language as it is. Second, the change that we imagine may sometimes be so radical, so queer, that it seems almost impossible to decide what adjustments might naturally be called for to accommodate it — the choice may seem quite impossibly open. Third, there may very well be some cases in which, however elaborately we describe some imagined situation, we may still feel that we do not know what such a situation would be *like*, and hence do not feel able to pronounce on what it would be natural to say or to do in that situation. However, we must not be pessimistic about this. The task of explaining why our concepts should be as they are may be intricate and perplexing, but it will not be the less interesting for that. Certainly there is no reason to believe — indeed there is reason *not* to believe — that this explanatory work is impossible. Not much such work has yet been done, and no doubt in course of time this whole family of problems will be seen in a clearer light than can be expected at the moment.

Finally, a few words about the inventive aspect of philosophical imagination. The situation here is, in a way, the converse of that which we have just considered. Instead of testing the concepts we actually employ by imagining how they might be modified if the facts were otherwise than they are, we may suppose the facts to remain unchanged but the concepts that we employ to be different. In other fields invention of this kind is not unfamiliar; it is essentially what Copernicus did in astronomy, or Einstein in physics; they were important, that is, not as the discoverers of new facts, but as the inventors of new ways of looking at old facts. The post-Copernican astronomer was not in possession of new truths about the heavens, but of a new conceptual system for organizing the truths he possessed already. Now, you may remember that Mr. Strawson referred to this kind of invention as the 'metaphysical' aspect of philosophy; and I think there are very good reasons for doing so. What has often seemed so queer about some metaphysicians is that, while what they say about the world is apt to seem perfectly extraordinary, it has a surprising way of coinciding with our ordinary beliefs. Take Berkeley, for example, who so vehemently denied the existence of matter. Even when all allowance has been made for the errors of his predecessors and his own eccentricities of vocabulary, it is impossible not to feel that his general picture of the world is very odd indeed; and yet at no point can it be brought into head-on conflict with our ordinary convictions — indeed, Berkeley represents himself, plausibly enough, as wishing to pick no quarrel whatever with the plain beliefs of all plain men. The explanation of this odd situation is, I think, that Berkeley was a metaphysician in just the sense that is in question here —

his doctrines, that is, did not consist essentially in the assertion of new beliefs or the rejection of old ones, but consisted rather of a kind of re-description, a shift of view-point, a modification of modes of thought. He saw the same world that the rest of us see, but saw it from a rather different angle. It ought, of course, to be remembered that this is not all that Berkeley himself would have claimed. He did not think of himself as inventing simply a *new* way of looking at the world, but rather as expounding the *right* way, the only way in which one sees things as they really are. But this, I think, is only to say that he, like other metaphysicians, had his illusions. The builders of such imaginative systems have always been prone to claim, not that they were inventing something new, but that they were discovering something real, penetrating the disguises of Reality. But such claims are fatal as well as unfounded. For it was precisely by making these claims, by presenting themselves as super-scientists, discoverers *par excellence*, that metaphysicians drew on their own heads the formidable bludgeon of Logical Positivism. Of course there was much misunderstanding here. It was often and justly urged that the Positivists had mistaken, or disregarded, the actual character of their adversary; but this was due in large measure to the fact that their adversary, the metaphysician, had habitually presented himself in false colours. A metaphysical system, an invented conceptual apparatus, may have many virtues, such as elegance, simplicity, originality, comprehensiveness, depth, or the power to give psychological satisfaction; but the claim that any such system is exclusively true, or uniquely faithful to Reality, is a claim which sets metaphysics on quite the wrong ground, ground from which it is liable to be destructively expelled.

I would like to use up my remaining time by repeating some old points and adding some new ones. First of all I ought to repeat a warning I gave at the beginning, though briefly. To distinguish in the way we have been doing between four types of philosophical activity, labelled therapeutic and systematic analysis, and explanatory and inventive imagination, should not be understood to imply that any one of these either is or could be quite separately pursued. On the contrary, each is apt not only to accompany but actually to involve the others. To resolve a paradox or dilemma occasioned by conceptual distortion requires that the distortion be corrected, and if we are to get the facts really right, not just right enough to yield some temporary relief, the necessary examination of concepts must be pursued in a manner at least in some degree systematic. Again, one of the best ways to trace out the anatomy of our concepts, to distinguish what is essential in them from what is merely peripheral, is to enquire how they would function in a variety of imaginary circumstances. The work of analysis is not wholly unimaginative, and the imagination cannot be profitably exercised except from a reasonably secure analytic base. However, it remains of course quite true that the bent of a particular philosopher may incline him to some one path in preference to the others, and thus may impart a particular predominant character to his work.

Next, I hope I may be forgiven if I say some things that are glaringly obvious. My excuse is that even the obvious is often overlooked. First, I should like to say in very plain terms that I am not, nor is any philosopher of my acquaintance, a Logical Positivist. This is worth saying, obvious though it must be in the light of this series of lectures, because there has seemed to be a current belief that Logical Positivism is somehow the official doctrine of contemporary philosophy. There is, in fact, no such official doctrine; and it is even more certain, if possible, that Logical Positivism is not it. I hope that this series may have made it plain that contemporary philosophy is not a dogmatic, restrictive body of doctrines at all, but a common pursuit of illumination in certain fields. It is tiresome, though perhaps natural, that academic subjects tend to be thought of in terms of rival schools and groups, with rival heroes and leaders; let us avoid this habit altogether if we can, but if we cannot, at least let us avoid inflicting on the present the obsolete classifications of the past.

I believe that this matter is important enough to deserve, even at this late stage, a word or two of amplification. I suppose the most immediately striking feature of Logical Positivism was its iconoclasm, its short and apparently lethal way with the ponderous enigmas of metaphysicians. No doubt it was this particular feature which earned for the Positivists alike their popularity and their odium. To many their tight, restrictive aridities seemed miraculously to clear the air, while to others they appeared as a blind attack on many valuable and wholly respectable intellectual achievements. Now I think we should be careful not to patronize Logical Positivism too airily, nor should we be over-apologetic for its excesses. I believe that it could not easily be denied that in philosophy an unusually high proportion of what has been written, and indeed is written, could not unjustly be described as nonsense, and it is no service to anyone to pretend otherwise. At the same time, it happens to be true that the restrictive iconoclasm of Logical Positivism is quite alien to the spirit of philosophy today. In particular, its exclusive respect for science, mathematics, formal logic, and very plain facts is now generally admitted to be unwarranted. If any one thing is characteristic of contemporary philosophy, it would be precisely the realization that language has *many* uses, ethical, aesthetic, literary, and indeed metaphysical uses among them. There is no tendency to say 'You must not (or cannot) say that'; there is a readiness to appraise on its merits whatever may be said and for whatever purpose, provided only that something *is* said and words are not used idly.

If, even when this policy of tolerance is appreciated, there are some people who still wish to complain that philosophy does not meet their requirements, that they look up like hungry sheep and are not fed, it may perhaps be proper to ask them why philosophy *ought* to meet their requirements. Hungry sheep should not expect to be fed simply because they are looking up, for they may be looking up in the wrong direction. It is no reproach to the hedger and ditcher that he does not spend time on feeding the sheep, and the sheep in fairness should admit this.

One last word of warning. In coming to the end of this lecture we come also to the end of the present series, and I should like to reduce the impression of finality which this may convey. In describing any process of development it is only too easy to give the impression that, at the point where the description breaks off, the process described has somehow stopped as well, as if a terminus had been reached beyond which no further development is to be looked for. Indeed, in a way it is difficult *not* to do this; for one cannot know exactly what is going to happen next; and even the conviction that changes will occur is apt to be somewhat abstract and bloodless, expressed as it must be in quite general terms. But this historical parochialism can at least be officially discountenanced, however hard it may be in practice to shake it off. At least one can explicitly and vigorously disclaim the belief that the present state of things in philosophy leaves no room for development and progress, and recognize the very certain fact that all will not be exactly the same in ten or twenty or a hundred years' time. Excessive deference to the past, however sympathetic, may often be cramping and harmful; but an unapologetic deference to the future, however unhelpful it may be in the present, is certainly both prudent and becoming.

THE END

PRINTED BY R. & R. CLARK, LTD., EDINBURGH